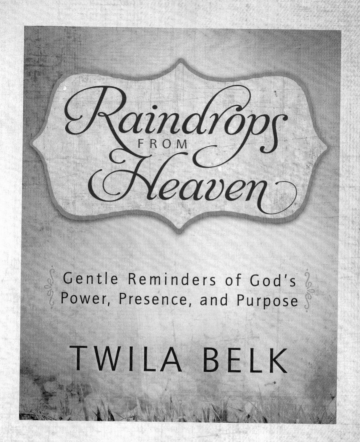

Raindrops FROM Heaven

Gentle Reminders of God's Power, Presence, and Purpose

TWILA BELK

BroadStreet
P U B L I S H I N G

BroadStreet Publishing Group LLC.
Savage, MN, USA
Broadstreetpublishing.com

Raindrops FROM *Heaven*

Gentle Reminders of God's Power, Presence, and Purpose
© 2015 Twila Belk

ISBN 978-1-4245-5615-1 (faux leather)
ISBN 978-1-4245-5013-5 (e-book)

Design by Chris Garborg | garborgdesign.com
Editorial services by Michelle Winger | literallyprecise.com

Printed in China.

18   19   20   21   22   23   24   7   6   5   4   3   2   1

*Let us acknowledge the L*ORD*;*

let us press on to acknowledge him.

As surely as the sun rises, he will appear;

he will come to us like the winter rains,

like the spring rains that water the earth.

HOSEA 6:3, NIV

Introduction

Years ago, while in the midst of bleak circumstances, I stared out the window and noticed the parched landscape due to a long-lasting drought. In my spirit I sensed God telling me, "Twila, the rain is coming. The rain is coming, and it's for you. Revel in the rain. Splash in the puddles. Delight in the deluge." God gives me that message often. It's one he wants to soak deep within my soul.

Rain has become symbolic to me of God's goodness and greatness. God speaks to me through the rain and reassures me of his love. I'm reminded of his power, presence, and purpose in my life.

Let the words in this devotional wash over you; allow them to saturate your mind and your heart. Meditate on the Scriptures at the top of each page. As you turn your thoughts to the truth of who God is and how great his love is for you, receive encouragement, hope, and comfort as you trust that God is big enough for all you need.

Dancing in the rain,

Twila

January

"You heavens above,
rain down my righteousness;
let the clouds shower it down.
Let the earth open wide,
let salvation spring up,
let righteousness flourish with it;
I, the LORD, have created it."

ISAIAH 45:8, NIV

January 1

ALPHA AND OMEGA

"I am the Alpha and the Omega—the beginning and the end,"
says the Lord God. "I am the one who is, who always was,
and who is still to come—the Almighty One"
(Revelation 1:8, NLT).

Almighty God, as the new year begins, I'm grateful that you are the Alpha and Omega, the A to Z in my life. You are—

Awesome and Amazing. Blesser and Burden bearer. Counselor, Comforter, and Caregiver. Defender, Deliverer, and Debt eraser. Eternal and Enough. Famous, Father, and Friend. Giver and Guide. Holy, Healer, and Helper. Indescribable and Incomprehensible. Jesus, Jehovah, and Joy giver. King of kings. Love, Light, and Life. Master, Messiah, and Miracle worker. Name above all names. Omnipotent, Omniscient, and Omnipresent. Promise giver, Promise keeper, and Provider. Quieter of my soul and Quilter of the pieces of my life. Redeemer, Revealer, and Renewer. Savior, Shepherd, and Shield. Truth. Unmatchable, Untouchable, and Undeniable. Valiant warrior and Victor. Wonderful, Worthy, and Wise. eXactly what I need. Yesterday, today, forever. Zealous.

You are my A-to-Z God for every day of the year, and thousands of pages could not contain all I have to say about you.

How is Almighty God the A to Z in your life?

January 2

EVERYTHING TO LIVE FOR

Praise be to the God and Father of our Lord Jesus Christ. In God's great mercy he has caused us to be born again into a living hope, because Jesus Christ rose from the dead. Now we hope for the blessings God has for his children. These blessings, which cannot be destroyed or be spoiled or lose their beauty, are kept in heaven for you. God's power protects you through your faith until salvation is shown to you at the end of time (1 Peter 1:3-5, NCV).

Yes, Father, because of Jesus I'm alive—truly alive. I can look beyond the darkness, pain, and disappointment of today and toward the future, knowing that you have everything under control and that nothing comes into my life without your concern and your provision.

Someday soon, I'll be healthy and whole and living a forever life with you in heaven. In the meantime, you've given me everything to live for and something to look forward to. The hope I have allows me to endure the here and now through your bubble of grace because I'm assured that the best is yet to come.

How does Jesus' resurrection change your life today?

January 3

SPIRITUAL BLESSINGS

All praise to God, the Father of our Lord Jesus Christ, who has blessed us with every spiritual blessing in the heavenly realms because we are united with Christ (Ephesians 1:3, NLT).

Father, I'm reveling in the rain, splashing in the puddles, and delighting in the deluge of your heavenly downpour in my life. You saturate my spirit with nourishment from above and give me everything I need for a strong, healthy, and productive life.

Thank you for the blessings of your power, presence, and purpose. I'm spiritually rich and overflowing with joy because of your goodness and love toward me.

What does being blessed with every spiritual blessing mean to you?

January 4

GOTTA TELL SOMEBODY!

The LORD is my strength and my song,
and he has become my salvation;
this is my God, and I will praise him,
my father's God, and I will exalt him
(Exodus 15:2, ESV).

Lord, the crescendo is building, and I can't contain the song in my heart. I have to brag on you, because the world—every person—needs to hear about my amazing God.

You are the reason I can sing when life is less than perfect. You are the one who gives me strength to put one foot in front of the other when the path before me is steep and full of twists and turns. You are the one who saves me from my enemy. You care about me. You intervene when I waver. You are at work in me, and through me, and for me, and I just gotta tell somebody!

Thank you for being my song, for making me strong, and for keeping me right where I belong—in your hands.

What kind of God do you have?

January 5

GIVER OF WISDOM

If any of you lacks wisdom, you should ask God, who gives generously to all without finding fault, and it will be given to you (James 1:5, NIV).

Lord, when tests and challenges come at me from all sides and I don't know what to do, I simply need to ask you for wisdom. You promise to give it to me in abundance. As I think about it, coming to you is the wisest thing I could do because you are the source of wisdom. I don't need a dozen degrees from a fancy university. I don't need a string of initials behind my name. I need only to get to know you better and learn to trust you more.

Help me appreciate the lessons you give me and the wisdom I gain through the trials I face. Thank you for allowing me to see things from your perspective.

For what circumstance do you need wisdom right now?

January 6

EPIPHANY

After this interview the wise men went their way. And the star they had seen in the east guided them to Bethlehem. It went ahead of them and stopped over the place where the child was. When they saw the star, they were filled with joy! They entered the house and saw the child with his mother, Mary, and they bowed down and worshiped him. Then they opened their treasure chests and gave him gifts of gold, frankincense, and myrrh (Matthew 2:9-11, NLT).

Jesus, you didn't give the wise men a map when they sought you. You gave them a star. How appropriate that a bright light would guide the wise men to you—the Light of the World! Being in the presence of the Light filled them with great joy.

Today, Lord, the joy of your presence in my life fills me with light. It illuminates my face and radiates from my eyes. People are drawn to the light within me and discover it's from you. Thank you for shining through me and for the joy that you give.

Are you filled with joy in Jesus' presence?

January 7
GREAT THINGS

"He alone has spread out the heavens
and marches on the waves of the sea.
He made all the stars—the Bear and Orion,
the Pleiades and the constellations of the southern sky.
He does great things too marvelous to understand.
He performs countless miracles" (Job 9:8-10, NLT).

God, you alone stretched the heavens across the canvas of the universe. They declare your glory. You alone strategically hand-placed the stars in the sky and provide their source of light. Their brilliant design speaks of your magnificence.

You alone created the mighty waters and control when they ebb and flow. You alone sustain all of creation since the beginning of time. You alone are capable of doing great things far beyond the boundaries of my comprehension. You alone have infinite wisdom.

This is a good reminder that you don't need my help in running your world.

Do you need to release control of something going on
in your life right now?

January 8

HE REJOICES OVER ME

The LORD your God is living among you.
He is a mighty savior.
He will take delight in you with gladness.
With his love, he will calm all your fears.
He will rejoice over you with joyful songs
(Zephaniah 3:17, NLT).

Lord, my soul dances with the reality that you have such strong feelings for me. I envision the glimmer in your eyes and the wide smile that brightens your face when you look upon me. I'm comforted by the warmth of your love as you hold me close to you. The songs you sing over me put a melody of praise in my heart.

You delight in me, love me, and rejoice over me. I feel it, Lord, and I'm in awe that the God of the universe would shine his favor on me the way you do. I delight in you, Lord. I love you, Lord. Because of your presence in my life, I rejoice.

How do you feel knowing that the God of the universe has such strong emotions for you?

January 9

HE'S WITH ME

"So do not fear, for I am with you;
do not be dismayed, for I am your God.
I will strengthen you and help you;
I will uphold you with my righteous right hand"
(Isaiah 41:10, NIV).

Father God, thank you for the assurance of your presence in my life. Thank you for being my God. Thank you for strengthening and helping me. Thank you for upholding me.

Because you are with me, I have no reason to fear. Because you are my God, I have confidence to face each day. Because you strengthen me and help me, I am courageous and competent. Because you uphold me with your right hand, I will not fall or fail. This I know to be true: you won't leave me; you won't stop being God; you won't release your firm grip on me.

Are you fearful or dismayed? Do you need strength and help?
How does this promise speak to you?

January 10

IN HIS ARMS

"I am the LORD your God
who takes hold of your right hand
and says to you, Do not fear;
I will help you" (Isaiah 41:13, NIV).

Lord, I wondered how you could take me by my right hand, yet uphold me with your righteous right hand at the same time. And then I realized the best way for you to do that would be to hold me in your arms!

When the storms of life threaten me, or when I face troubles of many kinds, I can reach up to my heavenly Father and know that you will pull me to your lap and into your big but gentle embrace. I lay my head on your breast, listen to your heartbeat, and realize that it's beating for me. With every pulsation, you communicate how loved I am.

For me, your arms are a place of comfort. A place of warmth. A place of rest. A place of contentment. A place of safety. A place of security. And you delight in keeping me there.

Do you need to sit on the Father's lap today?

January 11

COMPASSION

When he saw the crowds, he had compassion on them because they
were confused and helpless, like sheep without a shepherd
(Matthew 9:36, NLT).

Jesus, when you see crowds, you don't see a multitude of faces.
You see each person individually. You see the one who feels all alone,
even when she's in a crowd. You see the one who is defenseless.
You see the one who has fears. You see the one who feels insecure.
You see the one whose heart is heavy with grief. You see the one who
is confused. You see the one who needs help. You see the one who is
lost. And you have compassion on each one. Thank you for seeing
me in the crowd and knowing what I need.

How does Jesus' compassion affect you?

January 12

GOD'S PURPOSE

Many are the plans in a person's heart,
but it is the LORD's purpose that prevails (Proverbs 19:21, NIV).

Oh God, I could brainstorm a multitude of options for the course of my life. My first plans would probably be to remove the hurts, sorrows, heartaches, and hardships. That would make things easier for me. Then, of course, I would leave out the irritating people. They just cause problems. As my mind gets rolling, I come up with all kinds of ideas.

But when I stop to ponder how my ideas would impact me, I realize important truths. I wouldn't know joy without suffering. I wouldn't know peace without turmoil. I wouldn't know grace without trials. I wouldn't have a need for hope, and I wouldn't have a need to trust you. Without a need to trust you, I wouldn't know who you are. Thank you that your purposes, and not mine, prevail.

What are some of the options and plans you've
brainstormed for your life?

January 13

GOD IS NOT HUMAN

God is not a man, so he does not lie.
He is not human, so he does not change his mind.
Has he ever spoken and failed to act?
Has he ever promised and not carried it through?
(Numbers 23:19, NLT)

You're not a man, God. That's great news! Men lie, but you don't.
Your words are always sincere and never deceitful. Because you're not
human, you aren't wishy-washy or affected by hormones like I am.
You don't change your mind. If you say something is going to happen,
that's the way it is. Period.

You've never failed to act on your promises. I can count on you to
come through every time. I praise you for being my true, resolute,
and trustworthy God.

How does God's not being human impact you?

January 14

GRACE, LOVE, AND FRIENDSHIP

May the grace of our Lord Jesus Christ be with you all.
May God's love and the Holy Spirit's friendship be yours
(2 Corinthians 13:14, TLB).

Jesus, because of your amazing grace, I don't have to perform or live up to a certain set of standards. You haven't rejected me because of who I am or what I've done. Instead, you've showered me with kindness. Your grace empowers me, frees me, and causes my heart to leap with joy. I can't describe it, but I happily live in the reality of it.

Father, because of your extravagant love, I feel valued and cherished. Your desire to have a personal relationship with me sent Jesus to the cross to make it possible. The magnitude of that is hard for my mind to grasp.

Holy Spirit, because of your intimate friendship, I'm learning to appreciate and walk in the light of amazing grace and extravagant love.

Lord Jesus, Father God, and Holy Spirit—your beautiful, supernatural gifts are far beyond anything I deserve, and I'm grateful.

What is your response to God's grace, love, and friendship?

January 15

GLORIOUS FREEDOM

"The Spirit of the LORD is upon me,
for he has anointed me to bring Good News to the poor.
He has sent me to proclaim that captives will be released,
that the blind will see,
that the oppressed will be set free,
and that the time of the LORD's favor has come" (Luke 4:18-19, NLT).

Jesus, you carry the keys to my freedom and the promise of better things to come. Yet so many things try to hold me captive. The fear of tomorrow. The guilt of my past. Shame and regret. The expectations of others. My stinking thinking. The lies of the enemy. All these things blind me to the truth of your Good News.

The truth is that you have a plan for my life. The truth is that the road to liberty is paved with grace and hope for my future. The truth is that your authority can release the shackles from my feet so I can dance. The truth is that I have a choice—I can remain a prisoner, or I can be set free. I choose glorious freedom.

What's your choice?

January 16

POWER OF GOD

I am not ashamed of this Good News about Christ. It is the power of God at work, saving everyone who believes—the Jew first and also the Gentile (Romans 1:16, NLT).

Jesus, the good news about you is a lighthouse for those who need direction. A safe place for those who are abused. A hospital for the hurting. A treasure chest for those in need. A key that unlocks prison doors. A story that changes lives. A fountain of life-giving water. A muzzle that silences demons. How can I be ashamed of a message that brings healing, forgiveness, salvation, joy, peace, hope, freedom, and life?

I am not ashamed of this good news. Why? It is the power of God at work, saving everyone who believes—and that includes me.

How has the good news about Christ transformed you?

January 17

He Holds Things Together

He is before all things, and in him all things hold together
(Colossians 1:17, NIV).

Lord, I like the feeling of having it all together, and I like to be in control. But no matter how hard I try, my life at times seems to spin wildly out of alignment. Not only do I lose my sense of power, but I get dizzy too. My circumstances and the people around me are unmanageable, and the world as I see it appears to be spiraling downhill quickly.

Thank you for releasing me from the heavy burden and false notion that I need to keep the earth revolving on its axis, because I fail miserably at it. And thank you for the reminder that you were in existence before all things. You alone created all things. You alone control all things. You alone hold all things together. I'm glad that all things, including me, are in your hands.

What is something you're trying to control
that should be left in God's hands?

January 18

DIVINE INTERRUPTIONS

*You intended to harm me, but God intended it for good to accomplish
what is now being done, the saving of many lives (Genesis 50:20, NIV).*

God, you gave Joseph lofty dreams, and all evidence pointed to a
promising future. Yet a big interruption in plans seemed to change
everything. He had serious family issues. He was abandoned, sold
into slavery, and had to start over in a new land with a different
language. He was mistreated, lied about, imprisoned, and forgotten.
His integrity was compromised. He was a victim of other people's
agendas, and his circumstances were out of his control.

Years went by and the dreams appeared to vanish. But look what
you accomplished when everything seemed hopeless! You promoted
Joseph from prisoner to prime minister and through him you saved
his entire nation from demise!

As with Joseph, you can use divine interruptions in my life to groom me
into the kind of person you want me to be. They aren't always pleasant,
convenient, or easy, but you can use them to accomplish great things.

*How has God used the interruptions
in your life to groom you?*

January 19

LORD GOD ALMIGHTY

He who forms the mountains,
who creates the wind,
and who reveals his thoughts to mankind,
who turns dawn to darkness,
and treads on the heights of the earth—
the LORD God Almighty is his name (Amos 4:13, NIV).

Lord God Almighty, your name is great and you do great things. You formed the majestic mountains. Their beauty, size, and structure point to a powerful God. You create the wind. I can't see where it begins or ends, but I know when it's at work. It comes as a mighty force or as a gentle breeze and points to a powerful God. You turn dawn to darkness. Daytime and nighttime are under your control, and that points to a powerful God. You tread on the heights of the earth. Your footprint points to a powerful God.

I revere you—the all-powerful God—and I'm in awe that you would turn your attention to me. You choose to reveal your thoughts to me. You desire a relationship with me. I'm not insignificant to you. That's a big wow.

How do you feel knowing that God Almighty
wants a relationship with you?

January 20

WISDOM AND POWER

"Praise be to the name of God for ever and ever;
wisdom and power are his.
He changes times and seasons;
he deposes kings and raises up others.
He gives wisdom to the wise
and knowledge to the discerning.
He reveals deep and hidden things;
he knows what lies in darkness,
and light dwells with him" (Daniel 2:20-22, NIV).

I praise you, God, for you have wisdom and power far above that of presidents and kings and mighty human empires. You are the supreme ruler and have all authority. I'm thankful that even when the state of world affairs looks dark, you are not surprised because light dwells with you. You are able to steer the course of governments and nations. You will have your way in your time.

Lord, pour out your wisdom, knowledge, and discernment on the leaders of this earth. Reveal deep and hidden things to them and cause them to revere you. Show them your ways, oh Lord. Teach them your paths. Guide them in your truth.

Are you able to trust God's sovereignty?

January 21

IMPENETRABLE EMBRACE

I am convinced that nothing can ever separate us from God's love.
Neither death nor life, neither angels nor demons, neither our fears for
today nor our worries about tomorrow—not even the powers of hell can
separate us from God's love. No power in the sky above or in the earth
below—indeed, nothing in all creation will ever be able to separate us
from the love of God that is revealed in Christ Jesus our Lord
(Romans 8:38-39, NLT).

Jesus, I'm comforted knowing that absolutely nothing can get to
me when I'm in your embrace. Absolutely nothing can put a wedge
between your love and me. Your hugs are impenetrable. Although evil
forces come against me, people are cruel to me, heartaches challenge
me, and unthinkably difficult trials work to convince me that a loving
God wouldn't allow such things, I remember your promises.

You promised I'd have trouble, and you promised that you'd always be
with me. The troubles only cause me to lean harder and cling tighter to
you. As I grab hold, your outstretched arms pull me in and lock around
me. I rest near your heart, under your wing. You are my shelter, my safe
place, my savior, my keeper. Nothing compares to your embrace.

What is trying to get between you and God's love right now?

January 22

You watched me as I was being formed in utter seclusion,
as I was woven together in the dark of the womb.
You saw me before I was born.
Every day of my life was recorded in your book.
Every moment was laid out
before a single day had passed (Psalm 139:15-16, NLT).

Creator God, you were there. You intricately wove all my parts together with your own hands. You watched over me. You saw every move I made. You recorded every day of my life. You laid out every moment. And you did it all before I was born.

As I reflect on that, I realize these important truths: I am loved; I am wanted; I am valued; I have a divine purpose; my life is not an accident; and you created me fearfully and wonderfully to do things no one else can do. I may seem insignificant to myself or to others, but in your eyes I will always have great worth.

Do you realize your value to God?

January 23

THE LOST SHEEP

"If a man has a hundred sheep and one of them wanders away, what will he do? Won't he leave the ninety-nine others on the hills and go out to search for the one that is lost? And if he finds it, I tell you the truth, he will rejoice over it more than over the ninety-nine that didn't wander away! In the same way, it is not my heavenly Father's will that even one of these little ones should perish" (Matthew 18:12-14, NLT).

Loving Shepherd, sometimes in my quest to find greener pastures, I stray off the path and head in the wrong direction. My aimless wandering takes me further away from you, and I feel desperate without my leader and protector nearby. When you notice I'm missing, you search until you find me, and without rebuke hoist me on your shoulder and carry me home to safety.

You bear the heavy load for the joy of rescuing your lost sheep. It's just like when you bore the weight of my sins on the cross. What great love!

How do you feel when you're lost?

January 24

HIDDEN TREASURE

"I will give you treasures hidden in the darkness—secret riches.
I will do this so you may know that I am the LORD" (Isaiah 45:3, NLT).

Lord, I thank you for the dark times in my life because it's during
those times I uncover secret riches—the truth of who you are.
I value the gold nuggets you've given me. Here is what I discovered:

You will never abandon me. Your arms are long. You answer prayer.
Your grace is sufficient. You know me better than I know myself.
You know just what I need. You are Jehovah Jireh, my provider.
You love me more than anything I can imagine. You are creative.
You are rarely in a hurry, but you're always right on time. There's
nothing too big for you to accomplish. There's nothing too small for
your attention. You are who you say you are. You keep your promises.
You never change.

I've learned that the key to unlocking treasure is focus. Instead of
dwelling on the darkness, I need to keep my eyes on you.

What gold nuggets of truth have you uncovered?

January 25

NAME ABOVE ALL NAMES

God elevated him to the place of highest honor and gave him the name above all other names, that at the name of Jesus every knee should bow, in heaven and on earth and under the earth, and every tongue declare that Jesus Christ is Lord, to the glory of God the Father (Philippians 2:9-11, NLT).

Jesus, I struggle to put into words what your name means to me. It's the sweetest name I know. It changed my life and continues to transform me. Thank you.

What impact does the name of Jesus have on you?

January 26

POWER, LOVE, AND SELF-DISCIPLINE

The Spirit God gave us does not make us timid, but gives us power,
love and self-discipline (2 Timothy 1:7, NIV).

Lord, you've given me a job to do, but I'm wimpy, lack self-assurance, and feel inadequate for the task. Waves of fear and doubt roll over me, and I become intimidated by the silliest things. How I thank you for not expecting me to operate in my own strength! That would lead to failure. Instead, you've given me Holy Spirit power that enables me to do things far beyond my ability. I can move forward in the unwavering strength, confidence, and courage that come from you.

Thank you for that power. Thank you for the gift of love that helps me to reach out to other people and impact their lives. Thank you for self-discipline that helps me persevere. You've equipped me with everything I need to accomplish great things for you.

In what situation do you need the Holy Spirit's power?

January 27

KEEPS LAMP BURNING

You, LORD, keep my lamp burning;
my God turns my darkness into light (Psalm 18:28, NIV).

Lord, when my life seems dark because of the troubles that surround me, I can count on you to light a pathway for me. As I focus on you, I see clearly that your way is perfect, even if it brings me through dismal and dangerous valleys. I see that you are always with me, guiding me and protecting me. And I see how much you care for me because I trust in you.

Your light keeps me from stumbling and falling and keeps me moving forward. I can see hope at the end of the path. You, O Lord, keep my lamp burning; you turn my darkness into light.

When have you needed God to turn your darkness into light?

January 28

GOD'S PLANS

"For I know the plans I have for you," says the LORD. "They are plans for good and not for disaster, to give you a future and a hope" (Jeremiah 29:11, NLT).

Lord, I know you have a purpose and a plan for my life. You've revealed that to me in many ways. Before I was born, you had already recorded my days in your book. You have good plans for me, Lord, yet when I'm in the midst of circumstances that seem to derail those plans, I forget. You have good plans for me, Lord, yet when things don't happen in my timeframe, I get discouraged. You have good plans for me, Lord, and they are not the same plans as mine. Yours are better. For that I rejoice.

Thank you for your plans to prosper me in you. Thank you for your plans to draw me closer to you. Thank you for your plans to teach me about you. Thank you that your plans include an eternal future and a hope. Thank you for not giving up on your plans for my life.

What are God's plans for you?

January 29

INFINITELY BEYOND

Glory be to God, who by his mighty power at work within us is able to do far more than we would ever dare to ask or even dream of—infinitely beyond our highest prayers, desires, thoughts, or hopes
(Ephesians 3:20, TLB).

Lord, I often say that I run around barefooted because you constantly blow my socks off. You are amazing in what you do—far surpassing anything I could ever imagine. You are big enough to handle whatever I face, and you can use me in ways outside the realms of my wildest thoughts. You are infinitely beyond what society's rulebook tells me I have to do in order to succeed. You are infinitely beyond what anyone says is possible. You are not contained by people's words. You are not contained by human boundaries. The only thing that restrains you is limited thinking, limited belief.

You are able. You can do immeasurably more than anything I would ever dare to ask. And you're my God. Help me to align my thinking with the size of my God.

What big thing do you need God's help with?

January 30

GIANT SLAYER

*David replied to the Philistine, "You come to me with sword, spear,
and javelin, but I come to you in the name of the Lord of Heaven's
Armies—the God of the armies of Israel, whom you have defied.
"And everyone assembled here will know that the Lord rescues
his people, but not with sword and spear. This is the Lord's battle,
and he will give you to us!"
So David triumphed over the Philistine with only a sling and a stone,
for he had no sword (1 Samuel 17:45,47,50, NLT).*

Lord, young David's story is a great reminder for me that when
squaring off with my giants, I don't need to be equipped with an
illustrious education, the newest technology, the shiniest weapons, a
thousand-page giant-killer instruction manual, or well-trained military
reinforcements. If I move forward with an unwavering confidence in
my all-powerful God—the Lord of heaven's armies—there's no contest.
You are bigger than any overwhelming hurdle I face.

What are the giants you're up against right now?

January 31

STRONG AND COURAGEOUS

"Be strong and courageous! Do not be afraid and do not panic before them. For the LORD your God will personally go ahead of you. He will neither fail you nor abandon you" (Deuteronomy 31:6, NLT).

Oh God, heading into new territory can be terrifying, especially when I know there will be battles to face. But you empower me with strength and courage, and I'm able to be at peace because of your presence with me. Your promises have proven true in my life, so I can trust you to personally go ahead of me.

Not only will you lead the way, but you will also act as my shield and protector. You won't fail me. You haven't failed me yet, and because of your perfect track record I know it'll never happen. You won't abandon me. You have no intention of bailing out when things get tough. Instead, during those times you'll hold me close. I look forward to the exciting new things you have in store for me.

In what new territory do you need to trust God for strength and courage?

February

The LORD knows the days of the blameless,

and their heritage will remain forever;

they are not put to shame in evil times;

in the days of famine they have abundance.

PSALM 37:18-19, ESV

February 1

HE DIRECTS AND DELIGHTS

The LORD directs the steps of the godly.
He delights in every detail of their lives.
Though they stumble, they will never fall,
for the LORD holds them by the hand (Psalm 37:23-24, NLT).

Father, you've given me many wonderful opportunities, and I desire to serve you well. Help me to walk forward with everything you have for me without anything holding me back. Not fears or uneasiness or doubt.

I want to advance knowing I can trust your voice and that you will bring about what you said you would do. I want to move ahead without striving or stumbling. I want to rest in you, to be still, and to remember that you are God—the one who is directing my steps and walking beside me hand in hand. Thank you for delighting in every detail of my life.

Where is God directing you?

February 2

NO SHADOW

Those who look to him for help will be radiant with joy;
no shadow of shame will darken their faces (Psalm 34:5, NLT).

Lord, today is the day we hear a lot about shadows. Will the
groundhog see it or not? While that's a concern for some, of more
importance to me is that no shadow of shame will darken my face.
I want everyone I meet to see a shine rather than a shadow.

Your Word says that no one whose hope is in you will ever be put to
shame and that those who look to you are radiant. Because of your
forgiveness and love for me, I don't have to hang my head in shame
over the things I've done. I can look to you for help and know that
your light will remove any shadows that cloud my expressions. When
I spend time with you, it shows on my face. I radiate with joy, hope,
and acceptance.

Do others see a shine or a shadow on your face?

February 3
HE HAS NO EQUAL

Who has measured the waters in the hollow of his hand,
or with the breadth of his hand marked off the heavens?
Who has held the dust of the earth in a basket,
or weighed the mountains on the scales
and the hills in a balance? (Isaiah 40:12, NIV)

God, I'm in awe of your bigness. I'm unable to manage the dust in my house, yet you hold all the dust of the earth in a basket. Only a few teaspoons of water will fit in my hand, yet you measured all the waters of the earth in the hollow of yours. You marked off the heavens in the span between your thumb and little finger and weighed the mountains on scales. You contain and measure things that are uncontainable and immeasurable. You have no equal.

You are an immeasurably more God who can do things far above and beyond what I imagine. Thank you for the supernatural ways you are working in my life right now.

How does knowing that God has such big hands
make you feel?

February 4

POWERED BY THE SPIRIT

My message and my preaching were very plain. Rather than using clever and persuasive speeches, I relied only on the power of the Holy Spirit. I did this so you would trust not in human wisdom but in the power of God (1 Corinthians 2:4-5, NLT).

So often I feel inadequate for the things you've called me to do, yet you care more about my willingness and availability than about my ability to "put on a good show."

When I step forward in faith and rely on the Holy Spirit to work in me and through me, powerful things happen. Lives are changed, and you get the glory. Thank you, Lord.

In what area do you need the Holy Spirit's power?

February 5

MARVELOUS WORKMANSHIP

You made all the delicate, inner parts of my body
and knit me together in my mother's womb.
Thank you for making me so wonderfully complex!
Your workmanship is marvelous—how well I know it
(Psalm 139:13-14, NLT).

Loving Creator, your workmanship is marvelous. How well I need to remember it! Every day I'm bombarded with messages showing me and telling me that I need to look a certain way or act a certain way in order to have value. Thank you that the world's standards are not your standards.

You—the God of the universe—created me, and you did it in a wonderfully complex way. With great thought and care, you made all the delicate, inner parts of my body. As you knit me together in my mother's womb, you dreamed of the things I'd someday do that nobody else can do. Thank you for the reminder that nobody can do me like I can do me. I'm the only one of my kind.

How can you celebrate your uniqueness today?

February 6

SWEET PERFUME

Thanks be to God! For through what Christ has done, he has
triumphed over us so that now wherever we go he uses us to tell
others about the Lord and to spread the Gospel like a sweet perfume.
As far as God is concerned there is a sweet, wholesome fragrance in
our lives. It is the fragrance of Christ within us, an aroma to both the
saved and the unsaved all around us (2 Corinthians 2:14-15, TLB).

Jesus, your presence within me can't be hidden! The aroma fills the
air and changes the atmosphere wherever I go. Because of your
mercy and grace in my life, I have joy, peace, hope, and purpose—and
people are attracted to that. They want to know where they can get
the sweet perfume I'm wearing. And I have the privilege of telling
them about you. May I wear your fragrance well.

What fragrance are you wearing?

February 7

DIFFERENT FROM MOST

Then Jesus told the servants to fill them to the brim with water. When this
was done he said, "Dip some out and take it to the master of ceremonies."
When the master of ceremonies tasted the water that was now wine,
not knowing where it had come from (though, of course, the servants
did), he called the bridegroom over. "This is wonderful stuff!" he said.
"You're different from most. Usually a host uses the best wine first, and
afterwards, when everyone is full and doesn't care, then he brings out
the less expensive brands. But you have kept the best for the last!"
(John 2:7-10, TLB)

Yes, Jesus, you're different from most. Most people can't turn water
into wine. Most people can't take difficult circumstances and turn
them into something beautiful. Most people can't do the miracles that
you do. You're not just different from most—you're different from all.
And you're able to do "wonderful stuff" in my life.

What wonderful stuff would you like Jesus to do for you?

February 8

WISDOM AND REVELATION

I keep asking that the God of our Lord Jesus Christ, the glorious Father, may give you the Spirit of wisdom and revelation, so that you may know him better (Ephesians 1:17, NIV).

Father, you desire to have a relationship with me, but with my natural mind I can't understand your ways. How wonderful you are to provide everything I need to know you better!

Thank you for the way your Spirit connects with mine and reveals who you are. Thank you for the wisdom and clarity you give that helps me understand who Christ is and all he's done for me. Thank you for the intimate and personal ways you speak to me through your Spirit. Thank you that I can trust your voice. I know I'm loved.

Have you asked God for the Spirit of wisdom and revelation?

February 9

THE GREAT MULTIPLIER

He told the people to sit down on the grass. Jesus took the five
loaves and two fish, looked up toward heaven, and blessed them.
Then, breaking the loaves into pieces, he gave the bread to the
disciples, who distributed it to the people. They all ate as much as
they wanted, and afterward, the disciples picked up twelve baskets
of leftovers. About 5,000 men were fed that day, in addition to all
the women and children! (Matthew 14:19-21, NLT)

Jesus, this situation seemed impossible, but you took the five tiny
loaves and two small fish in your hands, blessed them, and fed
thousands of people. It's a great reminder of what you can do in the
impossible-looking, God-given situations in my life.

You have the power to supernaturally multiply time, resources, energy,
creativity, gifts, know-how, reach, efforts, generosity, harvest, or
whatever is needed. You are the great multiplier. I trust you to provide.

What do you need Jesus to multiply for you?

February 10

PERFECT PEACE

You will keep in perfect peace
all who trust in you,
all whose thoughts are fixed on you! (Isaiah 26:3, NLT)

Lord, as I focus on the things I'm facing, I become overwhelmed and I struggle to think about anything else. Fears, doubts, and forgetfulness of everything I know about you take over. But when my thoughts are fixed on you, I remember your faithfulness, goodness, and supernatural power. I remember that you are a God who loves and cares and provides. I remember that I can trust you, and perfect peace is mine.

What are your thoughts fixed on?

February 11

A WOW GOD

It is God who sits above the circle of the earth. (The people below must
seem to him like grasshoppers!) He is the one who stretches out the
heavens like a curtain and makes his tent from them
(Isaiah 40:22, TLB).

When it comes to you, God, WOW is about the only thing I can say
that makes sense. You are a WOW God. It's mind boggling to think
that the God of the universe—the God who created all things, the God
who sits above the circle of the earth and rules and reigns over all
things—allows me to approach him.

Even though I must seem to you like a grasshopper, you accept me.
I can talk with you freely and comfortably, and you respond.
You allow me to call you Father. You've chosen me as your child.
You've picked me to do your work. WOW! What a privilege it is
to love you and serve you.

What's your response to a WOW God?

February 12

GOD IS THE CREATOR

*God created mankind in his own image, in the image of God he
created them; male and female he created them (Genesis 1:27, NIV).*

Life-giving God, thank you that I'm not a product of a galactic
accident, a glob of ocean slime, or the relative of an animal I visit in
the zoo. You breathed life into me and created me in such a way that
I can commune with you. You gave me a personality—a mind to think
with, emotions to feel with, and a will to make choices. You gave me
a spirit that connects with your Spirit and allows me to know and
worship you. In you I live and move and have my being.

I'm grateful that although sin has marred my life, the redemptive
work of Jesus and the Holy Spirit's power are renewing your divine
nature within me daily. I'm a new creation!

*What are your thoughts about God's
masterful creation of you?*

February 13

PROCLAIM HIS NAME

Give praise to the LORD, proclaim his name;
make known among the nations what he has done.
Sing to him, sing praise to him;
tell of all his wonderful acts.
Glory in his holy name;
let the hearts of those who seek the LORD rejoice.
Look to the LORD and his strength;
seek his face always (1 Chronicles 16:8-11, NIV).

Oh Lord, your name is great and greatly to be praised. I will shout it from the rooftops and broadcast it far and wide! You are Creator God. Sustainer God. Provider God. Self-sufficient God. Healing God. Life-giving God. Abundant God. Above-and-beyond God. Immeasurably-more God. Amazing God. Sweet-surprises God. Blessing God. Wise God. Trustworthy God. Faithful God. Deliverer God. Upholding God. Shepherding God. Guiding God. Saving God. Loving God. Caring God. Big God. Strong God. All-in-all God.

Because you are All-of-the-above-and-much-much-more God, I will look to you and your strength. I will seek your face always.

How will you proclaim God's name?

February 14

No Greater Love

"There is no greater love than to lay down one's life for one's friends"
(John 15:13, NLT).

Jesus, this is how I know you love me:

You always have time for me. You listen to me and give your full attention to me when I talk. You enjoy hanging out with me. You want me to draw closer to you. You share intimate moments with me. You shower me with hugs and kisses every day. You delight in me. Your eyes light up when you see me. You whisper tender messages in my ear. You do nice things for me. You keep an eye on me. You hold me in your arms when I've had a hard day. You write love letters to me. You carry my name over your heart. You send me sweet surprises to remind me that you're thinking about me. You talk to your Father about me often. And you died to give me life. There is no greater love.

On this Valentine's Day, I'm glad I'm yours and you are mine.
I love you.

How has Jesus showed his love to you?

February 15

PURPOSE FULFILLER

I cry out to God Most High,
to God who will fulfill his purpose for me (Psalm 57:2, NLT).

God Most High, thank you for listening when I cry out to you. Thank you for gently reminding me that you haven't forgotten about the hopes, dreams, purposes, and plans you have for me.

At times it seems as if I'm in a stalled place, that there's an invisible barrier holding me back from doing the things you have for me to do. I get frustrated at not being able to move forward. But just because things look that way doesn't mean you're not still at work behind the scenes. You're doing things that I'm not aware of to make the way straight for what you have in store for me to do. You will fulfill your purposes for me. For that I'm grateful.

What is God's purpose for you?

February 16

"Blessed are those who trust in the LORD
and have made the LORD their hope and confidence.
They are like trees planted along a riverbank,
with roots that reach deep into the water.
Such trees are not bothered by the heat
or worried by long months of drought.
Their leaves stay green,
and they never stop producing fruit"
(Jeremiah 17:7-8, NLT).

Lord, I'm blessed to have you as my God. You are trustworthy and true. I can put my hope and confidence in you because you've proven yourself again and again.

I don't have to fear the heat of the pressures, stress, and troubles in my life right now because you are the source of living water, and my roots grow deep in you. With you there is no drought. My leaves are always green: a direct result of abiding in you. I can bear much fruit because you and you alone are my provider and sustenance.

Are your roots firmly planted?

February 17

HE IS GOD

"I have revealed and saved and proclaimed—
I, and not some foreign god among you.
You are my witnesses," declares the LORD,
"that I am God" (Isaiah 43:12, NIV).

Lord God, I have daily evidence in my life that you are God. No other god could do the things you do. No other god reveals himself in creation. No other god discloses divine truth through his written words. No other god has a Holy Spirit that makes known his will. No other god saves his people from demise. No other god proclaims good news of great joy for his people. No other god speaks and makes things happen. No other god cares about his people or communes with his people the way you do, Lord.

I am a witness that you and you alone are God.

What have you witnessed God do?

February 18

HE GETS IT

Since he himself has gone through suffering and testing, he is able to help us when we are being tested (Hebrews 2:18, NLT).

You get it, Lord. You get it. You know what it's like to face temptation. You know what it's like to be tired, hungry, and thirsty. You know what it's like to be poor. You know what it's like when people constantly want your attention. You know what it's like to have demands and pressures put on you.

You know what it's like to be misunderstood and mistreated. You know what it's like when people tell lies about you. You know what it's like to have people mock you. You know what it's like to be despised, rejected, and falsely accused. You know what it's like to be surrounded by people who are evildoers. You know what it's like to lose a loved one. You know what it's like to suffer. You know what it's like to face death. You know what it's like to be human. You can identify with me. And you know how to intercede on my behalf.

How does this encourage you?

February 19

O Lord, you have examined my heart
and know everything about me (Psalm 139:1, NLT).

Lord, I'm comforted in knowing that nothing on my heart gets past you. You know my longings and concerns. My wants and needs. My heartaches. My shortcomings. My thoughts. My frustrations. You are aware of everything about me, and you understand me better than I understand myself.

At times I can't express what's going on within me—things stir in me subconsciously and cause my emotions to fluctuate—yet even then, you get it. You can interpret the language of my heart. You see all things, God. You know me inside and out because you created me. You were with me in my mother's womb, and you're with me now.

What's on your heart right now?

February 20

GOD'S CREDENTIALS

Moses said to God, "I am not a great man! How can I go to the king
and lead the Israelites out of Egypt?"
God said, "I will be with you. This will be the proof that I am sending
you: After you lead the people out of Egypt, all of you will worship me
on this mountain" (Exodus 3:11-12, NCV).

Oh God, I can relate to Moses in so many ways. I make excuses.
I waver. I think about my lack of qualifications. I tell myself there's
no way I can do what you're asking. And then you remind me that
it doesn't matter who I am; it matters who you are.

You don't require competence or a long list of impressive credentials on
my part. You simply want my willingness and obedience. When I combine
that with your competence and your credentials, you always come
through with your end of the deal. And you are glorified in big ways.

What is God calling you to do that
requires his credentials and competency?

February 21
EVERYONE WHO CALLS

Everyone who calls on the name of the Lord will be saved
(Acts 2:21, NIV).

Lord, within these words lies great hope. Everyone who appeals to you for salvation will be saved. Everyone. It doesn't matter who they are or what they've done. If they come to you with earnest desire, believing in your name and trusting you, you will deliver them.

This is a reminder that you want to save and that you have a plan to save. You don't want people to perish without knowing you. It's also a reminder that I shouldn't give up praying for loved ones or neighbors or co-workers or people who seem to be beyond hope.

For whose salvation are you praying?

February 22

ABLE TO SOAR

Even youths will become weak and tired,
and young men will fall in exhaustion.
But those who trust in the LORD will find new strength.
They will soar high on wings like eagles.
They will run and not grow weary.
They will walk and not faint (Isaiah 40:30-31, NLT).

Lord, I get tired of flapping my wings. The harder I flap, the more exhausted and less effective I become, and it seems as if I get nowhere. I'm learning that you don't want me to strive or to try doing things in my own strength.

If I position myself with you, I can glide above the circumstances that wear me down. I can soar to new heights. When I trust in you, I will find new strength. I will not grow weary. I will not faint.

Are you flapping or soaring?

February 23

TOUCH OF FAITH

Just then a woman who had suffered for twelve years with constant bleeding came up behind him. She touched the fringe of his robe, for she thought, "If I can just touch his robe, I will be healed." Jesus turned around, and when he saw her he said, "Daughter, be encouraged! Your faith has made you well." And the woman was healed at that moment (Matthew 9:20-22, NLT).

Jesus, she was a hurting woman who took a risk and reached out for you because she knew you had the power to change her life. One woman in a multitude, and you felt her touch. It wasn't a touch like the others pressing in around you. It was the touch of faith.

That's all it took. Immediately you stopped everything and turned your attention to her. You treated her lovingly, with tenderness and compassion, and gave her something to live for. That's the way you treat everyone who reaches out to you in faith. You are a loving, tender, compassionate God.

How did your life change when you reached out to Jesus in faith?

February 24

A God-made Day

This is the day the Lord has made.
We will rejoice and be glad in it (Psalm 118:24, NLT).

Yes, Lord, I will rejoice, because you are a day-to-day God.
Today I'm grateful for many things—
Doors of opportunity. New things. Creativity. Provision. Your
purposes and plans. Your faithfulness. That you are God and I'm not.
Forgiveness. Your friendship. Guidance and direction. Favor. Your
healing touch. Compassion. Love. The way you smile at me. The way
you speak to me. Peace and joy. Promises given and promises kept.
The power of your Word. Truth. Hope. Your long arms. Sweet surprises.
Your presence. Laughter. Your amazing handiwork. Revelation,
knowledge, wisdom, discernment, insight, and understanding.
Those who have gone before me and have shown me the way. Your
sovereignty. Good news of great joy—a Savior who is Christ the Lord.
Tomatoes.

I'm grateful that I will never run out of things to be grateful for.
There's no end to your goodness. No end to your daily blessings.

For what things will you rejoice today?

February 25

LEVEL PATHS

*"I will make my mountains into level paths for them.
The highways will be raised above the valleys"* (Isaiah 49:11, NLT).

Lord, when I look at the mountain in front of me, I'm overwhelmed at the thought of climbing it. And usually it's not just one I'm staring at but an entire range. As I move closer to the mountain, I notice the tunnels you've provided that will take me through to the other side. Similarly, when I'm in the valley, you don't leave me there. You've provided a bridge over the valley that connects me with your highway.

Your grace is like a tunnel through my mountains and a bridge over my valleys. It's sufficient to get me through.

*How have you experienced God's grace
in the mountains or valleys?*

February 26

UNFORCED RHYTHMS OF GRACE

"Come to me, all you that are weary and are carrying heavy burdens,
and I will give you rest. Take my yoke upon you, and learn from me;
for I am gentle and humble in heart, and you will find rest for your
souls. For my yoke is easy, and my burden is light"
(Matthew 11:28-30, NRSV).

I love the sound of your invitation, Lord. Coming to you is like coming
to a spa for the soul. Your promise of recovery and rest makes me
want to say, "Aaahhhh."

Thank you for easing my load and for teaching me the dance steps
to the unforced rhythms of grace. When I slip into my old habits of
trying to do things my way, send me another invitation. I want to
keep company with you and to live freely and lightly.

Is it time for you to visit God's spa for the soul?

February 27
SUCCESSFUL PLANS

Commit your actions to the LORD,
and your plans will succeed (Proverbs 16:3, NLT).

Lord, sometimes I get caught up in what looks like a great idea and I jump in without giving it a second thought. Because of my creative mind, the ideas keep coming, but when I try to do everything I dream up, I become overwhelmed. Other times people ask me to take on projects because they know I can do them and do them well. I often say yes out of guilt or wrong motives.

You're teaching me a lesson I need to remember: I could save myself a lot of grief and unnecessary work if I would discuss my plans with you before carrying them out. If I align myself with your will and commit my actions to you, I will succeed. When it's of you and for you and through you, you will make it happen.

What project do you need to get God's thoughts about?

February 28

GOD OF HOPE

May the God of hope fill you with all joy and peace as you trust in him,
so that you may overflow with hope by the power of the Holy Spirit
(Romans 15:13, NIV).

God, bad news, heartache, pain, sorrow, trouble, and despair pervade the world around me, and I could easily get sucked into feelings of hopelessness. Instead, you've lightened my load by making me a carrier of hope.

Because I trust in you, I'm filled to the brim with supernatural joy and peace. It spills out of me and people notice. Then I get to tell them that the hope isn't because of anything I've done—it's all about what you've done in me and for me. It's the power of your presence in my life. Thank you that your spigot of hope never runs dry.

Are you allowing the Holy Spirit to fill you
to overflowing with hope?

February 29

MY HEART LEAPS

The LORD is my strength and my shield;
my heart trusts in him, and he helps me.
My heart leaps for joy,
and with my song I praise him (Psalm 28:7, NIV).

My heart leaps for joy, Lord, because you are my strength and my shield. My heart leaps for joy because you are my helper, and you've proven your trustworthiness again and again. My heart leaps for joy because of all you've done in my yesterdays and for all you will do in my todays and tomorrows.

I delight in you, Lord. I will extol your name at all times, and your praise will always be on my lips.

What makes your heart leap for joy?

March

Ask the LORD for rain in the spring,

for he makes the storm clouds.

And he will send showers of rain

so every field becomes a lush pasture.

ZECHARIAH 10:1, NLT

March 1

MARVELOUS LOVE

See how very much our heavenly Father loves us, for he allows us to be
called his children—think of it—and we really are! (1 John 3:1, TLB)

What marvelous love you've extended to me, God, and what joy I
experience calling you *Father!* I cherish the way you sing over me, and
I delight in singing praises back to you. I'm glad you never tire of that.
When I need a boost, you're my best cheerleader. Your daily assurance
and encouragement keep me moving forward. If I'm having a bad day,
you wrap your comforting arms around me and wipe the tears from my
eyes. You pull me onto your big lap, which is my favorite place to rest.

You know exactly what I need and when I need it, and that even
includes your discipline—because you want what's best for me.
As much as I fail, you never condemn. You just gently guide me back
to your good graces. I'm blessed to be a member of your family.
I'm honored to be your child.

What does being a child of God mean to you?

March 2

VICTORY

"See, God has come to save me.
I will trust in him and not be afraid.
The Lord God is my strength and my song
he has given me victory" (Isaiah 12:2, NLT).

Thank you, God, for coming to save me. You show up when I need it most and give me strength to face whatever is before me. You remind me that I have no reason to fear when you're around.

When I look to you and place my trust in you, you give me victory over anything I'm afraid of. Your presence brings perfect peace. You are my strength, you are my song, and you give me victory.

Over what fears do you need victory?

March 3

Call to Me and I will answer you and show you great and mighty
things, fenced in and hidden, which you do not know (do not
distinguish and recognize, have knowledge of and understand)
(Jeremiah 33:3, AMP).

God, every day with you is fresh and full of *Aha!* moments. You are
beyond understanding, yet you reveal great and mighty things as I get
to know you better and draw closer to you. I love that you sometimes
disclose important truths as I'm sleeping or meditating on you. And at
other times you'll make your secrets known through experiences I have
or people you set on my path. Thank you for trusting me with them!

I don't want to miss out on anything you have for me, Lord.
Open my spiritual eyes and enable me to see all you want me to see.
I long for more and more of you.

What great and mighty things has God revealed to you lately?

March 4

Everything that was written in the past was written to teach us,
so that through the endurance taught in the Scriptures and the
encouragement they provide we might have hope (Romans 15:4, NIV).

Lord, thank you for the encouragement I receive from the words in your Scriptures. You've preserved them to teach me important lessons about who you are and what you're able to do. You've shown me that when you're on the scene, nothing else matters.

You are the same God today that you were when the ancient words were written. That gives me great hope.

Which stories in the Bible give you hope?

March 5

No Need to Understand

Trust in the Lord with all your heart;
do not depend on your own understanding.
Seek his will in all you do,
and he will show you which path to take (Proverbs 3:5-6, NLT).

Lord, thank you for reminding me that I'm not supposed to
understand everything nor do I have a need for understanding
everything. That thought gives me great freedom because many
details in my life are beyond the realm of my mental grasp.

I don't understand the heartaches in my life. I don't understand
the decisions people make. I don't understand why things happen
differently than the way I think they should happen. But what I do
understand is this: you say I should trust you and seek your will in all
I do. If I follow your directions, you promise to show me which path
to take. You will take care of me. I'm not left to flounder on my own.
That gives me great comfort.

Are you depending on your own understanding or on God?

March 6

HEMMED IN

You hem me in, behind and before,
and lay your hand upon me.
Such knowledge is too wonderful for me;
it is high; I cannot attain it (Psalm 139:5-6, ESV).

God, as I think of how you position yourself on my behalf,
I'm reminded of the prepositions I learned in grade school.

You are before me and behind me, above me and below me, around
me and in me. You hem me in with your reassuring presence, whether
I'm coming or going. It's a wonderful thing to ponder. Thank you for
being my prepositional God.

What prepositions do you think of
when you ponder God's presence?

March 7

LEADER, TEACHER, SAVIOR

Show me your ways, LORD,
teach me your paths.
Guide me in your truth and teach me,
for you are God my Savior,
and my hope is in you all day long (Psalm 25:4-5, NIV).

Lord, I want to walk in your ways, not mine. I want to be on your paths. Thank you for guiding me in your truth and teaching me. Thank you for wisdom, discernment, revelation, knowledge, and insight that help me as I move forward. Thank you for accompanying me on the journey.

I trust you to reveal your desires and plans for me. You are God my Savior, and my hope is in you all day long.

In what areas do you need direction?

March 8

HIS TENDER WATCH-CARE

Come, let us worship and bow down.
Let us kneel before the LORD our maker,
for he is our God.
We are the people he watches over,
the flock under his care.
If only you would listen to his voice today! (Psalm 95:6-7, NLT)

Oh God, I'm like a sheep that is dependent on a shepherd. I have no sense of direction, and I'm defenseless against the predators that would enjoy a piece of me. Thank you for your tender watch-care over me. Not only do you guide and protect me, but you feed, clothe, and provide as well.

When I wander off the right path or fall prey to harmful things, you get my attention and tell me what to do for my safety's sake. Where would I be without you? You are worthy to be worshiped and adored, for you are my God, my maker, and my loving shepherd.

In what ways are you dependent on the Shepherd?

March 9
EVERLASTING GOD

Do you not know?
Have you not heard?
The LORD is the everlasting God,
the Creator of the ends of the earth.
He will not grow tired or weary,
and his understanding no one can fathom (Isaiah 40:28, NIV).

Lord, I want to shout to the world, "Do you not know? Have you not heard? Can't you see? Haven't you experienced the greatness of the everlasting God?" I want to tell people what I know to be true about you.

You are God and always will be. There is none like you—not even close. You are the one, true, living God. You are the creator of the ends of the earth, and you are the God who sustains all of creation. And if that's not enough, you are the God who works on my behalf. You are the God who saves, who loves, who cares for everything I need. You give, you pour out, you bless, you nurture, you amaze. And you don't grow tired or weary. It's hard for my human mind to fathom.

What do you think people need to know
about the everlasting God?

March 10

Helper of the Fatherless

But you, God, see the trouble of the afflicted;
you consider their grief and take it in hand.
The victims commit themselves to you;
you are the helper of the fatherless (Psalm 10:14, NIV).

Thank you, Father God, for seeing what's going on in my life. Nothing gets past you. When my grief and pain are unbearable, your heart hurts with mine. You understand how it feels, and you know just what to do to help me through it.

As I look to you for my safe-keeping, you shelter me, feed me, nurture me, provide for me, love me, strengthen me, and support me. I can rest in the security of your big arms.

How has the Father helped you in times of affliction?

March 11

A NEW HEART

"I will give you a new heart, and I will put a new spirit in you.
I will take out your stony, stubborn heart and give you a tender,
responsive heart" (Ezekiel 36:26, NLT).

God, thank you for the new heart and Spirit you gave me through
Jesus. It's an extraordinary gift that came at an exorbitant price.
I know that a new heart isn't available unless someone dies,
and Jesus happily became the donor for mine.

Before I received my new heart, my life held no hope, and nothing
I tried to do on my own would fix the problem. But thanks to Jesus,
I'm now transformed! I have great joy, wonderful peace, and a bright
future ahead of me. I have something to live for! I'm grateful for your
beautiful act of love.

How has your new heart transformed your life?

March 12

APPROACHABLE GOD

In him and through faith in him we may approach God with freedom and confidence (Ephesians 3:12, NIV).

God, at times when I'm busy, I get frustrated if the phone rings or people need me. I don't want to stop everything I'm doing just to listen to what they have to say. So when I think about you—the God of the universe, the creator of all things, the ruler of heaven and earth—who welcomes me into your presence at any time, I'm humbled and amazed.

With you I don't need an appointment and I don't have to wait in line. I have instant access. I can come to you boldly and with confidence, knowing that you won't reject me and that you'll hear whatever is on my heart. Not only do you give me your full attention, but you enjoy communicating with me as well. May I never forget what a remarkable privilege it is to approach you.

How do you feel knowing that the God of the universe is approachable?

March 13

The Destroyer

The Son of God came to destroy the works of the devil
(1 John 3:8, NLT).

Jesus, you—the innocent babe in the manger—were actually the destroyer. That's a huge thought to ponder. Your whole purpose in coming to earth was to completely defeat and invalidate the works of the devil. The devil is a snake, a deceiver, and a big fat liar, but thanks to you, I have truth to counter his lies. I have discernment to combat his deceptive tactics. I have light to expose his evil ways.

I praise you, Jesus, because you are the destroyer, and the devil is the defeated one. Hallelujah! Thank you for giving me the tools to remind him.

What's the defeated one trying to tell you?
What does the destroyer have to say?

March 14

I AM

God said to Moses, I AM WHO I AM and WHAT I AM, and I WILL BE WHAT I WILL BE; and he said, you shall say this to the Israelites: I AM has sent me to you! God said also to Moses, This shall you say to the Israelites: The Lord, the God of your fathers, of Abraham, of Isaac, and of Jacob, has sent me to you! This is My name forever, and by this name I am to be remembered to all generations (Exodus 3:14-15, AMP).

Father, when you call yourself I AM, you're really saying, "I AM sufficient. I AM faithful. I AM the God of details. I AM the God of the impossible. I AM always with you. I AM your provider. I AM your strength. I AM your shield. I AM your hiding place. I AM your all in all. I AM love. I AM life. Besides that, I AM all-knowing and I AM ALL-POWERFUL. I AM."

When you say I AM, you mean right now. Always present. Today. Thank you for being my right-now God.

What does I AM mean to you?

March 15

POURING OUT

"I will pour water on the thirsty land,
and streams on the dry ground;
I will pour out my Spirit on your offspring,
and my blessing on your descendants" (Isaiah 44:3, NIV).

Oh Lord, as my spirit thirsts for you, I can hear you saying, "The rain is coming. The rain is coming. The rain is coming, and it's for you, Child. Revel in it. Splash in the puddles. Delight in the deluge. Dance in the flash floods of my blessings."

You pour out your Spirit and I'm refreshed. Renewed. With every raindrop I'm reminded of your power, presence, and purpose. As you fill my life to overflowing, the blessings fall on my offspring and descendants. Thank you for your heavenly downpours and the joyful expectation they bring.

Have you experienced the rain?

March 16

GREAT LOVE

For God so greatly loved and *dearly prized the world that He [even]
gave up His only begotten (unique) Son, so that whoever believes
in (trusts in, clings to, relies on) Him shall not perish (come to
destruction, be lost) but have eternal (everlasting) life.
For God did not send the Son into the world in order to judge (to
reject, to condemn, to pass sentence on) the world, but that the world
might find salvation and be made safe and sound through Him
(John 3:16-17, AMP).*

God, you loved and prized me so dearly that you gave up Jesus,
your only Son. Because I made the decision to believe in him,
I'm not separated from you now or in eternity. I have everlasting life!
You didn't send Jesus to condemn me but so I could be saved, safe,
and sound through him.

Thank you for sending Jesus to hell on my behalf to cancel my
reservations there. That's the greatest act of love I'll ever know.

Do you understand how much God loves you?

March 17

REMINDERS

Joshua explained again the purpose of the stones: "In the future,"
he said, "when your children ask you why these stones are here and
what they mean, you are to tell them that these stones are a reminder
of this amazing miracle—that the nation of Israel crossed the Jordan
River on dry ground! Tell them how the Lord our God dried up the river
right before our eyes and then kept it dry until we were all across!
It is the same thing the Lord did forty years ago at the Red Sea!
He did this so that all the nations of the earth will realize that Jehovah
is the mighty God, and so that all of you will worship him forever"
(Joshua 4:21-24, TLB).

Mighty God, I love telling the stories of your goodness and
faithfulness in my life because they help me remember.
When I recall what you've done for me in the past, I can trust you
for today and tomorrow.

Thank you for your amazing works on my behalf.
I delight in worshiping you.

What reminders do you have of God's goodness?

March 18

IMPOSSIBLE?

With God nothing is ever impossible and *no word from God shall be without power* or *impossible of fulfillment (Luke 1:37, AMP).*

God, nothing is ever impossible for you. You are a big God. That's truth. You brought forth the Savior of the world through a virgin womb. You raised the dead back to life. Impossible things for anybody but you. A second truth is that you are able to do impossible things in partnership with willing and available people. Countless recorded events throughout history make that clear.

God, I'm willing. I'm available. May it please you to do limitless and amazing things in me and through me for your honor, glory, and praise.

What impossible things does God want to do
in partnership with you?

March 19

BIG ARMS

"He reached down from heaven and rescued me;
he drew me out of deep waters.
He rescued me from my powerful enemies,
from those who hated me and were too strong for me.
They attacked me at a moment when I was in distress,
but the LORD supported me.
He led me to a place of safety;
he rescued me because he delights in me"
(2 Samuel 22:17-20, NLT).

Loving God, your big arms reach down and scoop me up when I can't seem to get my head above water. Your big arms reach down and rescue me when I'm facing strong opposition. Your big arms reach down and support me when my troubles threaten to knock me down. Your big arms reach down, lift me up, and gently wrap me in your safe embrace. You hold me close because you delight in me. And I delight in you.

What have God's big arms done for you?

March 20

HIS PRESENCE

The LORD replied, "My Presence will go with you, and I will give you rest." Then Moses said to him, "If your Presence does not go with us, do not send us up from here (Exodus 33:14-15, NIV).

God, the words of Moses resonate deep within my soul. You have important things for me to do, but I'm apprehensive about what's ahead. I wouldn't have the courage to move forward without knowing that your presence is with me.

When you're with me, I don't have to strive to accomplish things in my own strength. You lead me, help me make decisions, and show me the right paths to take. You give me favor with those I encounter. You make a way for impossible things to happen. In your presence is shelter and safety. In your presence is freedom from fear. And in your presence is rest. Thank you for promising to go with me.

How does being in God's presence help you?

March 21

A New Thing

"Forget the former things;
do not dwell on the past.
See, I am doing a new thing!
Now it springs up; do you not perceive it?
I am making a way in the wilderness
and streams in the wasteland" (Isaiah 43:18-19, NIV).

New things are on the horizon, Lord. Shoots and sprouts are breaking through the soil. Buds are emerging. And I see hope springing forth wherever I go. Your long-awaited promise will be in full bloom soon. Really, really soon.

Yes, I know it takes a while for new things to grow—and it has seemed like forever—but the roots are taking a firm hold now and the blossoms are beginning to open. Their delightful fragrance is wafting through the air. I smell it, Lord. I perceive it. It's springing up! The new thing you've promised me is almost here! It's beautiful, Lord. Beautiful! My soul rejoices.

What's the new thing you've been awaiting?

March 22

FAITHFUL GOD

The faithful love of the LORD never ends!
His mercies never cease.
Great is his faithfulness;
his mercies begin afresh each morning
(Lamentations 3:22-23, NLT).

I praise you, oh Lord, for your unstoppable faithfulness and love.
I'm grateful that regardless of the many changes, hardships,
unknowns, and uncertainties in my life, I can count on you
to be a consistent, compassionate God.

I rejoice that your mercies begin afresh each morning.
Your goodness knows no end. All of my days hold great promise
and hope because your steady and reliable presence is with me.
You never change; you never fail.

How have you experienced God's faithfulness?

March 23

His Thoughts

"My thoughts are nothing like your thoughts," says the Lord.
"And my ways are far beyond anything you could imagine.
For just as the heavens are higher than the earth,
so my ways are higher than your ways
and my thoughts higher than your thoughts" (Isaiah 55:8-9, NLT).

Your thoughts and your ways are far beyond my comprehension, God. I don't understand why I experience pain, but your ways are higher than my ways. Some of the things you ask me to do make no sense at all to me, but your ways are higher than my ways. Many things about my life baffle me, but your ways are higher than my ways.

If I could read your mind, decipher your intentions, and figure out the way you work, I wouldn't need you. I'm grateful that you're God and I'm not. I can trust you to show up in every situation and to work in ways beyond my imagination.

What are some of the things you don't understand?

March 24

HEALER

News about him spread all over Syria, and people brought to him all who were ill with various diseases, those suffering severe pain, the demon-possessed, those having seizures, and the paralyzed; and he healed them (Matthew 4:24, NIV).

Jesus, you are the healer. You were the healer when you walked the earth. You were the healer throughout history. And you are the healer today. I can't refute the countless witnesses who testify to the amazing miracles you've done in their lives. You haven't changed.

Because your ways are higher than my ways, I don't understand how you work or think. But without a doubt I know that those who come to you and put their trust in you experience your compassionate, life-transforming touch. I'm grateful for your powerful impact on me.

Where do you need Jesus' healing touch?

March 25

Birthing New Life

Mary asked the angel, "But how can this happen? I am a virgin."
The angel replied, "The Holy Spirit will come upon you, and the
power of the Most High will overshadow you. So the baby to be
born will be holy, and he will be called the Son of God. What's more,
your relative Elizabeth has become pregnant in her old age!
People used to say she was barren, but she has conceived a son
and is now in her sixth month" (Luke 1:34-36, NLT).

Amazing God, I'm in awe of you. Mary had a virgin womb, Elizabeth
had a barren womb, and you brought life through both! You're not
limited in what you can do. Because you work in supernatural ways,
you can bring life to hopeless situations. You can bring life to dormant
dreams. You can bring life to struggling ministries. You can bring
life to the neglected and abused. You can bring life to anything and
anyone! Thank you for being a life-giving God.

Where would you like to see God bring life?

March 26

UNFAILING LOVE AND COMFORT

I cried out, "I am slipping!"
but your unfailing love, O LORD, supported me.
When doubts filled my mind,
your comfort gave me renewed hope and cheer (Psalm 94:18-19, NLT).

Oh God, at times I feel as if I'm hanging on to a wimpy, rootless tree on the side of a cliff. I wonder how long I can hold on and whether the tree will bear my weight. But that's not the way it is when I turn to you. When I cry out, "I am slipping!" I don't have to fear the fall, because your unfailing love is there to support me.

When doubts fill my mind and cause me to waver in my purpose, you get my attention through a friend, an experience, or a verse that reminds me you haven't forgotten me. You comfort me and renew my hope. Thank you for giving me the courage and strength to hang on.

When have you felt like you were losing your grip?

March 27

WORTHY OF PRAISE

For great is the LORD and most worthy of praise;
he is to be feared above all gods.
For all the gods of the nations are idols,
but the LORD made the heavens.
Splendor and majesty are before him;
strength and joy are in his dwelling place
(1 Chronicles 16:25-27, NIV).

Nothing compares to you, Lord. No god is greater, no god is stronger, no god is higher than you. Of what worth is a dead god? And of what value is a god made by human hands? It doesn't communicate, it doesn't feel, it doesn't show compassion, it doesn't love, and it can't invent anything.

You are the living God who dwells with your children. Your presence brings strength and joy. And you are Creator God who is awesome in power. Your splendor and majesty fill the earth. I adore you, Lord! Only you are worthy of honor, glory, and praise.

For what will you praise God today?

March 28

GOD CAUSES GOOD

We know that God causes everything to work together for the good of those who love God and are called according to his purpose for them (Romans 8:28, NLT).

God, you don't say that everything is good for me. You don't say that everything is your will for me. You don't say that I'll never have troubles. But you do say that you can use everything in my life for good. When I reflect on my difficult experiences of the past, I see how you've used them for your glory. Your purpose wasn't for me to suffer, but you used the things that caused suffering in my life for good.

Thank you for how you've changed me. Thank you for how I've been able to help others because of what I've learned. Thank you for the deep truths I've realized about you. Thank you for the ministry I now have because of the way you work all things together for good. You've done beautiful things in me, through me, and for me, and that is according to your purpose.

How have you seen God work all things together for good in your life?

March 29

IN THE NAME OF THE LORD

Those who went ahead and those who followed shouted,
"Hosanna!"
"Blessed is he who comes in the name of the Lord!" (Mark 11:9, NIV)

Lord Jesus, you came to earth with an important job to do, and that was to save the world. You represented God the Father, and you are God, but you humbled yourself—coming in as a man, riding on a donkey—and became obedient to death on a cross. Because of that, you were exalted to the highest place and given the name that is above every name. And at your name every knee will bow, in heaven and on earth and under the earth, and every tongue confess that you are Lord, to the glory of God the Father. (See Philippians 2:6-11.)

Jesus, I bow before you and honor your name. You are my Savior. You are my King. You are my Messiah. You are my God. I am blessed because you came in the name of the Lord.

How are you blessed because of Jesus?

March 30

KINGDOM OF POWER

The kingdom of God is not a matter of talk but of power
(1 Corinthians 4:20, NIV).

Lord, what good are the words I say about you if I'm not willing to live them out? If I say I trust you, but then worry about the things I'm facing, where's the power? If I say you're a big God who can do anything and then live as if I don't believe it, where's the power? If I say you are strong when I am weak, what does it prove when I still try to do everything on my own? Where's the power?

If I want others to see you at work in my life, then I must be willing to be puny and humble and to go through trials so that your power will be displayed. Lord, help me to live as if I believe you are who you say you are. Help me to live as if I believe your words are true. And may you be honored and glorified in big ways.

What do you say about God? Are you living it?

March 31

GOD PROVIDES

"Don't lay a hand on the boy!" the angel said. "Do not hurt him in any way, for now I know that you truly fear God. You have not withheld from me even your son, your only son."
Then Abraham looked up and saw a ram caught by its horns in a thicket. So he took the ram and sacrificed it as a burnt offering in place of his son. Abraham named the place Yahweh-Yireh (which means "the LORD will provide"). To this day, people still use that name as a proverb: "On the mountain of the LORD it will be provided"
(Genesis 22:12-14, NLT).

Provider God, you have not withheld from me even your son,
your only son. On the mountain of the Lord, he was provided.

There is no greater sacrifice. No greater provision. Because you provided
Jesus on my behalf, I can trust you to provide anything else I need.

How has God provided for you?

April

I know that the LORD is great,

that our Lord is greater than all gods.

The LORD does whatever pleases him,

in the heavens and on the earth,

in the seas and all their depths.

He makes clouds rise from the ends of the earth;

he sends lightning with the rain

and brings out the wind from his storehouses.

PSALM 135:5-7

April 1

GOD'S FOOLISHNESS

The foolishness of God is wiser than human wisdom, and the weakness of God is stronger than human strength (1 Corinthians 1:25, NIV).

Yes, God, the things you do and the decisions you make seem mighty foolish. You consider a man who was a murderer and adulterer to be a man after your own heart. You included a prostitute in the genealogy of your son. You commissioned a guy with a speech impediment as your spokesperson. You used an old, childless man to become the father of nations. You brought forth the Messiah from a virgin womb. You saved the world through an innocent Lamb. You love people who hate you.

Your foolishness is wiser than human wisdom, and your weakness is stronger than human strength. With that kind of logic, it makes sense that you can use me. I'm honored to be part of your foolish plan.

What are some of the things God does
that make no sense to you?

April 2

PAID IN FULL

When he had received the drink, Jesus said, "It is finished." With that,
he bowed his head and gave up his spirit (John 19:30, NIV).

Jesus, everything in all of history boiled down to those three words:
"It is finished."

At that precise moment, death ended and life began.

You did what you came to do.

Thank you.

What impact do those three words have on you?

April 3

HE CARRIED MY WEAKNESSES

It was our weaknesses he carried;
it was our sorrows that weighed him down.
And we thought his troubles were a punishment from God,
a punishment for his own sins!
But he was pierced for our rebellion,
crushed for our sins.
He was beaten so we could be whole.
He was whipped so we could be healed.
All of us, like sheep, have strayed away.
We have left God's paths to follow our own.
Yet the LORD laid on him the sins of us all (Isaiah 53:4-6, NLT).

Jesus, they were my weaknesses. My sorrows. My rebellion. My straying ways. My sins. And for them you were pierced, crushed, beaten, and whipped.

Why? So I could be whole and healed. So I could have a relationship with the Father. So I could have life to the full.

You laid down your perfect life for me. Me! How can I keep from singing your praises?

What's your response to Jesus for what he did for you?

April 4

GONE FOREVER

He will wipe every tear from their eyes, and there will be no more death or sorrow or crying or pain. All these things are gone forever (Revelation 21:4, NLT).

Jesus, one day you will wipe every tear from my eyes. There'll be no more death, no more sorrow, no more crying, and no more pain. All those things will be gone forever. What a glorious promise and what great hope it gives me! I'll be surrounded by your glory, enraptured in your presence, and enjoying unfathomable peace and joy eternally.

How I look forward to the day I'm carried home to you! What a wonderful time of rejoicing that will be.

What are you looking forward to most about that day?

April 5

RISEN FROM THE DEAD

Then the angel spoke to the women. "Don't be afraid!" he said. "I know you are looking for Jesus, who was crucified. He isn't here! He is risen from the dead, just as he said would happen. Come, see where his body was lying. And now, go quickly and tell his disciples that he has risen from the dead, and he is going ahead of you to Galilee. You will see him there. Remember what I have told you." (Matthew 28:5-7, NLT)

Jesus, I can't prevent the hallelujahs from rising up within me!

You're not in the grave! Hallelujah!

Death couldn't hold you down! Hallelujah!

You rose again, just as you said you would! Hallelujah!

You're alive! Hallelujah!

And it's all because of you, I'm alive.

Hallelujah!

How does knowing Jesus is alive impact your life?

April 6

GREATNESS OF GOD'S POWER

I also pray that you will understand the incredible greatness of God's power for us who believe him. This is the same mighty power that raised Christ from the dead and seated him in the place of honor at God's right hand in the heavenly realms. Now he is far above any ruler or authority or power or leader or anything else—not only in this world but also in the world to come (Ephesians 1:19-21, NLT).

Jesus, you are far above any ruler, authority, power, or leader. You are far above anyone and anything in this world and in the world to come. And you offer the same life-giving, life-transforming, divinely dynamic power that raised you from the dead and seated you at God's right hand in the heavenly realms to me. That's mind boggling!

If I can get a grip on what that means to me, nothing can hold me back from doing the incredibly great things you have in store for me. May it be so, Lord. May it be so.

What does this mean to you?

April 7

STRENGTH OF MY HEART

My health may fail, and my spirit may grow weak,
but God remains the strength of my heart;
he is mine forever (Psalm 73:26, NLT).

Loving, faithful God, you are the strength of my heart. Circumstances
of life may beat me down. Troubles may knock the spirit out of me.
People may disappoint me or reject me. My heart may be broken.
My health may deteriorate. My inadequacies may confront me daily.
But no matter how physically or emotionally weak I am, you never fail.

When my weariness causes me to doubt your love or care for me,
you bolster me with gentle reminders of your goodness. As I dwell
on who you are, my heart is strengthened, and I always come back
to these truths: you love me; you care about me; you are my hope;
and you are mine forever.

How is God the strength of your heart?

April 8

His Kindness

Oh, put God to the test and see how kind he is! See for yourself the way his mercies shower down on all who trust in him (Psalm 34:8, TLB).

God, when I didn't know how I'd pay the bills, you delivered money to my mailbox. When I didn't know where my food would come from, you brought a meal to my doorstep. When I didn't have gas money and when I needed clothes, you provided gift certificates. When I was sad, you cheered me with tulips. When I was striving, you pointed out a butterfly. When my heart was burdened, you sent a friend. When people let me down, you reassured me of your faithfulness. When I didn't think I could face another day, you gave me strength. When my soul was parched, you watered it with rain.

You are a magnificent, wonderful, awesome, merciful, kind, unfailing God, and I trust you. You always come through for me.

What has God done for you when you've put him to the test?

April 9

LOVE DEMONSTRATED

God showed how much he loved us by sending his one and only Son into the world so that we might have eternal life through him. This is real love—not that we loved God, but that he loved us and sent his Son as a sacrifice to take away our sins (1 John 4:9-10, NLT).

God, you demonstrated your extreme love for me by sending Jesus. With every lash of the whip, with every blow of the hammer, with every drop of blood, your message was clear: you love sinners. But what baffles me, Lord, is the reason you did it.

You sent your one and only Son *so that* I might have eternal life through him. You wanted me to live with you forever! You wanted me to have a personal, intimate relationship with you before forever happened! For you to love me that much is incomprehensible. I'm humbled. And grateful. And so in love with you.

How does God's reason for sending Jesus impact you?

April 10

ABUNDANT LIFE

*The thief comes only in order to steal and kill and destroy.
I came that they may have and enjoy life, and have it in abundance
(to the full, till it overflows) (John 10:10, AMP).*

Lord, the thief's tool chest is always open, and he does whatever he can to rob me of joy, peace, and hope. But when I'm engaged with you, the thief's tactics can't harm me. Instead, they draw me to you. And the closer I am to you, the more vitality, purpose, and contentment I have. I get an infusion of abundant life, and the enemy's plans are thwarted. That's a big woohoo!

Jesus, you came to give life. You want me to enjoy life and have it to overflowing. It's truly possible with you! I can experience it today and throughout eternity. Thank you!

In what ways have you experienced abundant life?

April 11

THE FOUNT OF WISDOM

The Lord grants wisdom! His every word is a treasure of knowledge
and understanding. He grants good sense to the godly—his saints.
He is their shield, protecting them and guarding their pathway
(Proverbs 2:6-8, TLB).

Every word of yours is a treasure, Lord. I cherish the time I spend
seeking you in Scripture and the insights your Spirit gives me while
there. As I grow in knowledge of you, the more I understand your
transformational truths and the more I trust you. As I apply what
you've taught me, I gain wisdom. With the wisdom and good sense
you give me, you keep me safe and on the right paths.

Lord, you are the fount of wisdom, and you give it abundantly to
those who revere you. It's more precious than rubies and leads to a
full life. Thank you for such a valuable gift!

How has wisdom and good sense kept you safe
and on the right paths?

April 12

OUT OF THE MUD

I waited patiently for the Lord to help me,
and he turned to me and heard my cry.
He lifted me out of the pit of despair,
out of the mud and the mire.
He set my feet on solid ground
and steadied me as I walked along
(Psalm 40:1-2, NLT).

Dwelling on the negatives is a slippery slope to despair for me, Lord. The more I focus on them, the more I forget important truths about you. The more I lose my grip on those truths, the faster my downward fall into the pit of mud and mire. It's dark, lonely, and messy there, Lord, and I don't like it.

When I look up, I see light. I see you. If I call out and stretch my arms toward you, you turn to me and hear my cry. You pull me up and set me on solid ground. You steady me with reminders of who you are. Lord, help me to keep my eyes where they belong—on you.

How has dwelling on the negatives pulled you
into a pit of despair?

April 13

No Escaping

I can never escape from your Spirit!
I can never get away from your presence!
If I go up to heaven, you are there;
if I go down to the grave, you are there.
If I ride the wings of the morning,
if I dwell by the farthest oceans,
even there your hand will guide me,
and your strength will support me
(Psalm 139:7-10, NLT).

There's no escaping you, Lord. Wherever I am, you're there, and your Spirit is with me—always. That knowledge gives me great comfort. You see me. You know what's going on in my life. You know when I need guidance and strength. And you're there to make it happen.

Not only are you present and readily accessible for me, Lord, but you're also there for my loved ones who aren't with me. Even though they're out of my reach, they're not out of yours. I praise you for being the always-present, all-encompassing God!

What comfort do you receive knowing
you can't get away from God's presence?

GOD REMEMBERED

God remembered Noah and all the wild animals and livestock with him in the boat. He sent a wind to blow across the earth, and the floodwaters began to recede (Genesis 8:1, NLT).

God, you remembered Noah and you won't forget me!

My redemption draws near. The dove has returned with a budding olive branch in its mouth, the waters are receding, and soon I'll see dry land. First there'll be some mud, but then the land will be dry enough to walk on. Dry enough to let down the drawbridge. Dry enough to leave the stinky ark in which I've had to live for so long. Dry enough to walk among the flowering meadows of your perfect future. Dry enough to dig a new foundation for the next phase of my life.

Thank you that you never intended the ark to be my permanent home. Thank you for the hope of tomorrow.

What does God have in store for the next phase of your life?

CERTAINTIES

"Be sure of this: I am with you always, even to the end of the age"
(Matthew 28:20, NLT).

Lord, I often hear people refer to the famous quotation that in this world nothing can be certain except death and taxes. That statement is so wrong! The only thing in this world I can be certain of is *you* And here are some statements I know to be true about you—

You're with me always, even to the end of the age. You'll never forget me. You'll never leave me. You'll never reject me. You'll never stop loving me. You'll never fail me. And besides all that, with you, life is possible even after death and taxes.

Thank you that I can be sure of you and your promises.

What can you be sure of about God?

April 16

UNLIMITED RESOURCES

I pray that from his glorious, unlimited resources he will empower you with inner strength through his Spirit. Then Christ will make his home in your hearts as you trust in him. Your roots will grow down into God's love and keep you strong. And may you have the power to understand, as all God's people should, how wide, how long, how high, and how deep his love is. May you experience the love of Christ, though it is too great to understand fully. Then you will be made complete with all the fullness of life and power that comes from God (Ephesians 3:16-19, NLT).

Jesus, I will never fully understand the magnitude of your love for me, but I realize how valued I am, and that gives me great joy. I'm blessed that you received my invitation to make my heart your home. I want it to be a warm and welcoming place for you, so I need your help in making it that way.

Thank you for tapping in to your unlimited resources on my behalf to help me become all you want me to be.

How does God use his unlimited resources on your behalf?

April 17

HOLY SPIRIT HELP

I will ask the Father, and He will give you another Comforter
(Counselor, Helper, Intercessor, Advocate, Strengthener, and Standby),
that He may remain with you forever—The Spirit of Truth, Whom the
world cannot receive (welcome, take to its heart), because it does not
see Him or know and recognize Him. But you know and recognize Him,
for He lives with you [constantly] and will be in you
(John 14:16-17, AMP).

Holy Spirit, I praise you for your constant presence in my life. I rely
on you for strength when I'm weak. You empower me when I'm
inadequate for the jobs I need to do. When I can't pray, you intercede
on my behalf. You help me know the Father better by revealing his
heart to me. If I need guidance, you direct me. You enlighten me and
help me discern between right and wrong. You encourage, convict,
counsel, give confidence, bring reassurance, comfort, and remind.
You teach me truth and help me walk in it. I don't know what I'd do
without your help. What a gift you are to me!

What role does the Holy Spirit play in your life?

April 18

ALL AUTHORITY

Jesus came to them and said, "All authority in heaven and on earth has been given to me." (Matthew 28:18, NIV)

Jesus, you have all authority—without exception. By your authority, you created the heavens and the earth. You forgive sins. You heal the sick. You defeat the enemy. You beat the power of death.

You rule over all things, Jesus. You sustain all things. You have all things under your control. And you are with me always. Because of this, I can trust you. When I work in your name and under your authority, you empower me for whatever you ask me to do.

Who is your authority?

April 19

BLESSED AND EXALTED NAME

"Blessed be your glorious name, and may it be exalted above all blessing and praise. You alone are the LORD. You made the heavens, even the highest heavens, and all their starry host, the earth and all that is on it, the seas and all that is in them. You give life to everything, and the multitudes of heaven worship you"
(Nehemiah 9:5b-6, NIV).

I exalt you, my Lord. You deserve all blessing and honor and praise! Your name is glorious, for you alone are the everlasting-to-everlasting God. The heavens, the earth, and all that is in them—including me—came from you. You gave me life and breath, and I rejoice in the privilege of using my breath to worship you.

Your goodness knows no measure. You are a forgiving God, gracious and compassionate. You instruct me in your ways and guide me on your paths. You provide and sustain, and you do not abandon me. Thank you for being my God.

For what reasons do you praise and worship God?

April 20

EQUIPPER

May the God of peace—who brought up from the dead our Lord Jesus, the great Shepherd of the sheep, and ratified an eternal covenant with his blood—may he equip you with all you need for doing his will. May he produce in you, through the power of Jesus Christ, every good thing that is pleasing to him. All glory to him forever and ever! Amen (Hebrews 13:20-21, NLT).

Yes, Lord! May you equip me with everything I need for doing your will, and may you produce in me every good thing that is pleasing to you. I want to serve you well, and I want my life to bring you glory.

Thank you for your Word that guides me, and for the privilege of prayer. Thank you for the fellowship and help of others who love you, and thank you for suffering. I know that without it, I wouldn't have the depth of relationship I have with you today. It's all part of your equipping process. I praise you for the strengthening power of Jesus at work in me and for the peace you provide.

How is God equipping you for doing his will?

April 21

GOD'S BATTLE

"Listen, all you people of Judah and Jerusalem! Listen, King Jehoshaphat! This is what the LORD says: Do not be afraid! Don't be discouraged by this mighty army, for the battle is not yours, but God's"
(2 Chronicles 20:15, NLT).

Oh Lord, how I need these words! They give me great hope and freedom from the burden of so many ongoing battles. It takes a lot of energy and resources to fight, Lord, and I don't have the strength or stamina to keep it up. Right now I'm feeling squeezed on all sides. I have internal pressures, external pressures, and pressures upon pressures.

Thank you for being aware of what's going on in my life. Thank you that when I turn my attention to you, I'm reminded that the battles aren't mine, but yours. I don't have to be afraid. I don't have to be discouraged. Confidence, courage, and relief come from you—the one who fights for me.

What battles are you trying to face on your own right now?

April 22

ABUNDANT RAIN

"Listen, you heavens, and I will speak;
hear, you earth, the words of my mouth.
Let my teaching fall like rain
and my words descend like dew,
like showers on new grass,
like abundant rain on tender plants"
(Deuteronomy 32:1-2, NIV).

Lord, when I think of your teaching falling like rain and your words descending like dew, I remember the manna you provided for the Israelites. As with manna, and as with the rain, your words are essential for life. They provide nourishment. They are fresh for each day.

When your words descend on me, I'm renewed. I absorb them into my mind and heart, and before long the cares that cause me to wilt no longer bother me. Your teaching invigorates me and infuses me with strength. It helps my roots to grow deep and allows me to mature in you. As I allow your words to penetrate my life, I'm more healthy and fruitful. I delight in your abundant rain, Lord.

How has God's abundant rain helped you grow?

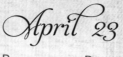

April 23

His Plans and Purposes

The plans of the Lord stand firm forever,
the purposes of his heart through all generations (Psalm 33:11, NIV).

Lord, no matter what happens, no matter how things look, your plans stand firm forever. The purposes of your heart stand firm through all generations. Even when my day goes differently than I had planned. Even when my life seems topsy-turvy. Even when the world is in chaos. None of that changes your purposes and plans.

Thank you for being a faithful God. Thank you for being a trustworthy God. Thank you that I'm in your hands.

When does it seem to you as if God's purposes
and plans are wavering?

April 24

HE OPENED A PATH

Moses raised his hand over the sea, and the LORD opened up a path through the water with a strong east wind. The wind blew all that night, turning the seabed into dry land. So the people of Israel walked through the middle of the sea on dry ground, with walls of water on each side! (Exodus 14:21-22, NLT)

Lord, I can relate with the Israelites right now. I'm in a place where you've obviously led me, yet I'm up against an impossible situation. I see no hope before me, and the enemy's at my back. Why would you bring me here after all we've gone through? You wouldn't quit on me, would you? Absolutely not! You promise to never abandon me.

You have a purpose and a plan for me. You're a loving God, not a cruel God. And you are creative. A hopeless situation for me is really just an opportunity for you to show your power. Thank you for your amazing plan that will open up a path for me. You will be glorified, and people will know that you are the Lord.

What impossible situation is before you right now?

April 25

POWER OVER WIND AND WAVES

Then Jesus got into the boat and started across the lake with his
disciples. Suddenly, a fierce storm struck the lake, with waves breaking
into the boat. But Jesus was sleeping. The disciples went and woke him
up, shouting, "Lord, save us! We're going to drown!"
Jesus responded, "Why are you afraid? You have so little faith!"
Then he got up and rebuked the wind and waves,
and suddenly there was a great calm.
The disciples were amazed. "Who is this man?" they asked.
"Even the winds and waves obey him!" (Matthew 8:23-27, NLT)

Jesus, you are Almighty God, the one who has ultimate authority.
Even the winds and the waves obey you! Because you are my God,
I don't have to dread the turbulent weather that threatens to capsize
me. When I look to you for help, you calm my nerves, remove my fears,
and speak tranquility into each situation I face. There is peace in
your presence.

What storms are rocking your boat?

April 26

HIS LARGENESS

Your steadfast love, O Lord, is as great as all the heavens.
Your faithfulness reaches beyond the clouds. Your justice is as solid as
God's mountains. Your decisions are as full of wisdom as the oceans
are with water. You are concerned for men and animals alike
(Psalm 36:5-6, TLB).

Wow, Lord! These are words that describe a big God: Love as great as the heavens, faithfulness that reaches beyond the clouds, justice as solid as mountains, wisdom as full as the oceans are with water.

I'm microscopic in comparison, yet not one part of my life escapes your awareness. You know my every thought, my every desire, and my every need, and you delight in caring for me. Thank you!

How do you feel knowing that none of your life slips
between the cracks with God?

April 27

STRENGTH FOR THE WEARY

He gives strength to the weary and increases the power of the weak
(Isaiah 40:29, NIV).

Oh God, I'm exhausted, and my burdens seem to get heavier with each day. I don't know how much longer I can go on. When I'm this weary, Lord, my mind starts playing tricks on me, and I forget these important truths: you are an everlasting God who doesn't grow tired or weary; you are an all-powerful God who gives strength to the weary and increases the power of the weak.

With your help, I'll have the stamina to accomplish far more than I ever thought possible. Thank you for the reminder.

How has God's strength helped you to carry on?

April 28

THE DONKEY SPEAKS

Then the LORD gave the donkey the ability to speak
(Numbers 22:28, NLT).

God, how I thank you for these powerful words! They give me great hope. If you can use a donkey to get your message across, you can certainly use me.

How does God want to use you?

April 29

THE VOICE OF THE LORD

The voice of the LORD is over the waters;
the God of glory thunders,
the LORD thunders over the mighty waters.
The voice of the LORD is powerful;
the voice of the LORD is majestic.
The voice of the LORD breaks the cedars;
the LORD breaks in pieces the cedars of Lebanon (Psalm 29:3-5, NIV).

Lord, I hear the rolling thunder, and it comforts me because your voice is there. It's full of wonder. And I feel safe. Your voice is majestic, Lord. It created the heavens and the earth and all things in it. You speak and storms are calmed.

Your voice is tender and compassionate, Lord. It beckons me and tells me I'm forgiven and loved. It speaks gently to my spirit. Your voice transforms lives, Lord. It commands lame people to rise up and walk and the blind to open their eyes and see.

History was changed forever when you proclaimed three little words: "It is finished." Your voice is powerful and glorious, Lord, and with my voice I will praise you.

How will you use your voice to praise him?

April 30

CLOSE TO HIS HEART

He tends his flock like a shepherd: He gathers the lambs in his
arms and carries them close to his heart; he gently leads those
that have young (Isaiah 40:11, NIV).

God, you've given me a beautiful picture of how you, as my loving
shepherd, pick up your little lamb—me—in your big, strong arms and
carry me near your heart. I can see the tender look on your face as
you gaze into my eyes, and I hear your heart beating out a love song
as my head rests against your breast. What warmth and security I feel
there! I'm able to rest without the cares and concerns of my world
distracting me. I know I'm safe and loved in your embrace, Lord.
Thank you for holding me close.

What picture does this verse bring to your mind?

May

My teaching will drop like rain;

my words will fall like dew.

They will be like showers on the grass;

they will pour down like rain on young plants.

May 1

WHOLEHEARTED LOOKING

"If you look for me wholeheartedly, you will find me"
(Jeremiah 29:13, NLT).

God, you don't play hide-and-seek with me. You're always findable.

If I search for you in creation, I'll find you.

If I search for you in Scripture, I'll find you.

If I search for you in prayer, I'll find you.

If I search for you in praise, I'll find you.

If I search for you in worship, I'll find you.

If I fully embrace the search, I'll find your full embrace.

Where are you finding God?

May 2

JOY OF THE LORD

*"Go and celebrate with a feast of rich foods and sweet drinks,
and share gifts of food with people who have nothing prepared.
This is a sacred day before our Lord. Don't be dejected and sad,
for the joy of the LORD is your strength!" (Nehemiah 8:10, NLT)*

Lord, as I rehearse the many ways you bless me and shower me
with love, the cares of the world that normally wear me down are
forgotten. Thinking about you changes my focus. My sadness and
discouragement are turned to joy, and hope fills my spirit.

You're teaching me that joy isn't the absence of sorrow or pain, but
it's your presence at work in my life. In your presence is fullness of joy,
and the joy I have in you instills me with strength. Thank you, Lord!

When have you experienced joy in the midst of sadness?

May 3

PEACE AND CONFIDENCE

I have told you these things, so that in Me you may have [perfect]
peace and confidence. In the world you have tribulation and trials
and distress and frustration; but be of good cheer [take courage; be
confident, certain, undaunted]! For I have overcome the world. [I have
deprived it of power to harm you and have conquered it for you.]
(John 16:33, AMP).

Jesus, you were right. The world is full of tribulation, trials, distress,
and frustration. If I focus on what's going on around me, or even
on what I'm experiencing in my own life, I become overwhelmed.
My thoughts spiral downward toward hopelessness.

If I turn my attention to you, the overcomer, my outlook changes.
The troubles are still there, but you deprive them of their power to
harm me. You give me peace and confidence to face each day.

How have you experienced peace and confidence during
troubling times?

May 4
NEVER FORGET

Let all that I am praise the Lord;
may I never forget the good things he does for me.
He forgives all my sins
and heals all my diseases.
He redeems me from death
and crowns me with love and tender mercies.
He fills my life with good things.
My youth is renewed like the eagle's! (Psalm 103:2-5, NLT)

Oh Lord, how I praise you for your goodness to me! Your mercies never end. You forgive my sins and remember them no more. You cast them as far as the east is from the west. You heal. You give life—abundant life. You favor me with your love.

Because you fill my life with good things, I have renewed energy and can soar. May I never forget who you are and what you've done in my life.

What are the good things God does for you?

May 5

POWER IN WEAKNESS

Each time He said, "My grace is all you need. My power works best in weakness." So now I am glad to boast about my weaknesses, so that the power of Christ can work through me. That's why I take pleasure in my weaknesses, and in the insults, hardships, persecutions, and troubles that I suffer for Christ. For when I am weak, then I am strong (2 Corinthians 12:9-10, NLT).

Jesus, you are amazing! Only you could take an inadequate person—me—and accomplish great things. When I get self out of the way and rest in your sufficiency, you show up and show off. You get the glory and not me—and that's where the glory belongs.

When has Jesus done great things through you despite your weaknesses?

May 6
JUST IN TIME

When we were utterly helpless, Christ came at just the right time and
died for us sinners. Now, most people would not be willing to die for
an upright person, though someone might perhaps be willing to die for
a person who is especially good. But God showed his great love for us
by sending Christ to die for us while we were still sinners
(Romans 5:6-8, NLT).

At just the right time you showed up, Jesus. You knew I needed help and that you were the only one who could provide it. It didn't matter to you who I was or what I'd done. You rescued me and accepted me because of who you are.

God, thank you for your incomprehensible act of love. You sent Christ to die for me while I was still a sinner. That's a big wow.

As you ponder what Christ did for you, how do you feel?

May 7
HE CARES FOR ME

Give all your worries and cares to God, for He cares about you
(1 Peter 5:7, NLT).

Lord, my burdens become too heavy for me to bear, so I'm thankful
for your daily invitation to give them up to you. You want all of my
worries and cares. Every. Single. One. Of. Them. So here they are:

Family matters, the choices my loved ones are making, financial
problems, lack of resources, my future, health issues, relationships,
deadlines, the pressure to perform, big decisions that affect my life, time
constraints, fears about safety, my insecurities, being vulnerable, the
temptations I face, the scary stuff happening in the world, the direction
of our nation, and many others that lay subconsciously on my heart.

Because I'm in good hands with my always-caring God,
I can trust you to carry my load.

What worries and cares do you need
to give to God right now?

May 8
HE GOES AHEAD

"Do not be afraid or discouraged, for the LORD will personally go ahead of you. He will be with you; he will neither fail you nor abandon you"
(Deuteronomy 31:8, NLT).

We've been here before, Lord. It's a message you're trying to get through my thick head. There's no reason for me to be afraid or discouraged.

It doesn't matter what I'm facing right now. You are with me. You are personally going ahead of me, and you have no plans to fail me or abandon me. Got it. Thanks for the reminder.

How can you apply this reminder to your circumstances today?

May 9
BLESSING

"May the LORD bless you
and protect you.
May the LORD smile on you
and be gracious to you.
May the LORD show you his favor
and give you his peace" (Numbers 6:24-26, NLT).

Father, your smile brings me great joy. I see the twinkle in your eye and the way your face brightens as you tell me how much you love me. Every day you shower me with kindness and blessings and remind me how favored I am.

When I bask in your presence, you bring a sweet calm to my spirit. I'm safe and warm there. How I delight in being your child!

How has your relationship with the Father blessed you?

May 10

SUN STANDS STILL

As the men of Israel were pursuing and harassing the foe, Joshua
prayed aloud, "Let the sun stand still over Gibeon, and let the moon
stand in its place over the valley of Aijalon!" And the sun and the
moon didn't move until the Israeli army had finished the destruction of
its enemies! This is described in greater detail in The Book of Jashar.
So the sun stopped in the heavens and stayed there for almost twenty-
four hours! (Joshua 10:12-13, TLB)

God, you control the sun and moon, and time is in your hands. That's
something I need to remember, especially when my heavy load of
responsibilities overwhelms me and there doesn't seem to be enough
hours in my day.

You may not choose to let the sun stand still as you did for Joshua,
but your power at work in me and in my situation can accomplish
more than I ever thought possible. You will provide whatever I need
for whatever I need to do today.

What time constraints are overwhelming you right now?

May 11
ALL THINGS

*All things were made and came into existence through Him; and
without Him was not even one thing made that has come into being
(John 1:3, AMP).*

You spoke and everything came into being, Lord. Trees that shade,
protect, and produce fruit. Vibrant hummingbirds, scampering
squirrels, and quirky turkeys. Rippling rivers and raging oceans.
Sandy beaches. Tulips, lilacs, and roses that fill the air with pleasant
fragrance. Exquisite landscapes and breath-taking horizons.
A sun that radiates with life-giving energy and warmth.
Raindrops that refresh and renew.

The whole earth and everything in it declares your majesty and
proclaims your glory, Lord. And you've given it for me to enjoy.
May I never lose the wonder.

How does God's creation speak to you about him?

May 12

PROMISE DELIVERED

Is anything too hard or too wonderful for the Lord? At the appointed time, when the season [for her delivery] comes around, I will return to you and Sarah shall have borne a son (Genesis 18:14, AMP).

God, nothing is too hard or too wonderful for you. You made that truth clear when 90-year-old, barren Sarah gave birth to her long-before promised child, Isaac. I need that reminder, Lord.

Sometimes I wait for what seems like forever for you to fulfill your promises to me. But you know the proper season for their fulfillment, and I don't. You haven't forgotten. You *will* return. And you *will* deliver hope, blessing, and promise regardless of my age or what I've gone through. You are a faithful God.

What does God want to birth through you?

May 13
POWERFUL COMPASSION

Soon afterward Jesus went with His disciples to the village of Nain, and a large crowd followed him. A funeral procession was coming out as he approached the village gate. The young man who had died was a widow's only son, and a large crowd from the village was with her. When the Lord saw her, his heart overflowed with compassion. "Don't cry!" He said. Then he walked over to the coffin and touched it, and the bearers stopped. "Young man," He said, "I tell you, get up." Then the dead boy sat up and began to talk! And Jesus gave him back to his mother (Luke 7:11-15, NLT).

Jesus, you couldn't contain your compassion for the widow and it spilled over to her dead son. Your compassion is powerful. It brings life. It gives hope. It restores dreams.
I praise you for being a compassionate, powerful God.

When has Jesus' compassion for you brought life, given hope, or restored a dream?

May 14
GOD RESPONDS

So they took the bull given them and prepared it. Then they called
on the name of Baal from morning till noon. "Baal, answer us!"
they shouted. But there was no response; no one answered. And they
danced around the altar they had made.
At noon Elijah began to taunt them. "Shout louder!" he said. "Surely
he is a god! Perhaps he is deep in thought, or busy, or traveling.
Maybe he is sleeping and must be awakened." So they shouted louder
and slashed themselves with swords and spears, as was their custom,
until their blood flowed. Midday passed, and they continued their
frantic prophesying until the time for the evening sacrifice. But there
was no response, no one answered, no one paid attention
(1 Kings 18:26-29, NIV).

Living, attentive God, I'm so grateful to have a relationship with you.
I don't worry whether you'll hear me because you're always wide-
awake, and you're aware of my every heart-whisper, whimper, or cry.
You're never too busy to act on my behalf. I love you.

How grateful are you to be in relationship with the living,
attentive God?

May 15
THE VINE

"I am the Vine; you are the branches. Whoever lives in me and I
in him shall produce a large crop of fruit. For apart from me
you can't do a thing" (John 15:5, TLB).

Jesus, you are my source of abundant life and the sustenance I need
to produce beautiful fruit for God's glory. When I abide in you, I take
on your characteristics. I'm able to:

love those who are unlovable,

be joyful when heavy burdens are crushing me,

experience peace when raging storms threaten to uproot me,

show patience when I want to wring someone's neck,

extend kindness and goodness when it's underserved and
unappreciated,

exhibit faithfulness even when others let me down,

give a gentle, caring touch to those who hurt or are in need, and

have the self-control to hold my strong will in check.

Thank you for working in me and through me, Jesus. I couldn't
produce a thing without you.

What fruit have you produced as a result of your
connection to the Vine?

May 16

LOOKS AREN'T EVERYTHING

The LORD said to Samuel, "Do not consider his appearance or his height.... The LORD does not look at the things people look at. People look at the outward appearance, but the LORD looks at the heart"
(1 Samuel 16:7, NIV).

Lord, how I praise you for not seeing me as the world sees me! The world puts value on the outward appearance, but you look at my heart. You value me because I seek after you.

The world values position; you say I'm royalty. The world values riches; you've made me a joint-heir with Jesus. The world values careers; you've made me your ambassador. The world values education; you've given me wisdom, knowledge, and understanding. The world values social standing; you've offered me a relationship with the King of kings and Lord of lords. The world values success; you've made it possible for me to do everything through Christ who gives me strength. I'm feeling pretty good about myself now, Lord. Thank you for my status in you.

What does God see when he looks at you?

May 17

NEW LIFE

Anyone who belongs to Christ has become a new person. The old life
is gone; a new life has begun! (2 Corinthians 5:17, NLT)

I love new things, Lord, and I rejoice that in you I'm a new person.

I have a new, tender heart. I no longer have a heart of stone.

I have a new perspective. I see people and your Word differently.

I have a new mindset. I'm equipped with truth to counter
the stinking thinking and lies.

I have new desires. I want to seek you and serve you with all my heart.

I have a new purpose—to bring honor and glory to you.

Thank you for your transformational power in my life.

How are you a new person in Christ?

May 18
A STRONG REFUGE

The LORD is good,
a strong refuge when trouble comes.
He is close to those who trust in him (Nahum 1:7, NLT).

Lord, I used to think I could control everything myself—that no matter what came at me, I was good enough, strong enough, and smart enough to manage on my own. But that didn't last long. Life gets tough, troubles pile up, and I realize my best isn't good enough to handle everything I face. I can't do it alone.

Thank you for showing me that you never intended it to be that way. You provide a place for me to go, and it's not hard to find. It's only a whispered prayer, a surrendered sufficiency away. I'm comforted knowing that when I trust you, you are there. You draw me close and gently remind me that I'm safe with you. You are good—a strong refuge when trouble comes. I'm grateful that you are close to me.

How is God your strong refuge?

His Ears Are Attentive

The eyes of the LORD are on the righteous,
and his ears are attentive to their cry (Psalm 34:15, NIV).

Lord, sometimes I'm with a group of people and no one seems to be aware that I'm there. A few might observe me from a distance, but they don't see my unreleased tears or hidden pain. All they see is the smile that masks my true feelings.

You keep an eye on me, Lord. You know about my secret sorrows and you comfort me. Your ears are attentive to my moans and groans, and you pick up even my unuttered cries. You're tuned in to my needs and you care. I might feel alone and neglected when I'm around others, but I know you're always with me, you're always faithful, and your love for me never fails.

How does it comfort you to know that God
is attentive to your cry?

May 20
THE MIRACLE

Very early the next morning, the king got up and hurried out
to the lions' den. When he got there, he called out in anguish,
"Daniel, servant of the living God! Was your God, whom you
serve so faithfully, able to rescue you from the lions?"
Daniel answered, "Long live the king! My God sent His angel
to shut the lions' mouths so that they would not hurt me, for I
have been found innocent in His sight. And I have not wronged you,
Your Majesty."
The king was overjoyed and ordered that Daniel be lifted from the den.
Not a scratch was found on him, for he had trusted in his God
(Daniel 6:19-23, NLT).

God, Daniel trusted in you, and you rescued him from the ferocious
lions. Likewise, when I trust in you, you deliver me from my
circumstances. Sometimes it's without a scratch; other times the miracle
is the grace that gets me through. People witness the peace and joy I
have, and they can't deny the power of the living God at work.

What evidences of the living God do people see in you?

May 21

GOD'S MASTERPIECE

We are God's masterpiece. He has created us anew in Christ Jesus,
so we can do the good things he planned for us long ago
(Ephesians 2:10, NLT).

You do beautiful work, Lord. Ever since I met Jesus, you've been fashioning me into your masterpiece—an exceptional creation. You've kept me in just the right environments so I would grow according to your plan, and through that you've uniquely shaped me to reach lives in ways others can't.

I see how you're weaving all the pieces of my life together to make me into the person I am today—a person you can use in big ways for your glory, honor, and praise. Thank you for what you're doing in me and through me.

What is the beautiful work God is doing in you?

May 22
THE PRODUCER

The Holy Spirit produces this kind of fruit in our lives: love, joy, peace,
patience, kindness, goodness, faithfulness, gentleness, and self-control.
There is no law against these things! (Galatians 5:22-23, NLT)

Holy Spirit, selfishness isn't your fruit, but love is. Somberness isn't
your fruit, but joy is. Anxiety and fear aren't your fruit, but peace is.
Restlessness and annoyance aren't your fruit, but patience is. Cruelty
isn't your fruit, but kindness is. Evil isn't your fruit, but goodness is.
Unreliability isn't your fruit, but faithfulness is. Harshness isn't your
fruit, but gentleness is. Impulsiveness isn't your fruit, but self-control is.
When I'm intimate with Jesus, you produce beautiful fruit in my life.

What kind of fruit are you bearing?

May 23
DEEP WATERS

He reached down from on high and took hold of me;
he drew me out of deep waters (Psalm 18:16, NIV).

Lord, I feel as if I'm drowning. I'm barely treading water and making no progress. It's not a comfortable feeling, and I'm doing the work you wanted me to do! I've thought about giving up several times—that I just can't do it. Then you remind me who you are. You remind me of the sermons I like to give others about your ability and faithfulness. Why is it easier to speak truth than to live it out?

Help me to hold on, Lord, and to remember that you will do whatever is needed to accomplish your will. If that plan involves me, you will strengthen and enable me through the Holy Spirit. You won't leave me powerless or hopeless. I praise you in advance for how you're going to reach down from on high and take hold of me. You will draw me out of deep waters. I love you, Lord, and I trust you to be God.

What deep waters are you in?

May 24

HOLY SPIRIT POWER

You will receive power when the Holy Spirit comes upon you. And
you will be my witnesses, telling people about me everywhere—in
Jerusalem, throughout Judea, in Samaria, and to the ends of the earth
(Acts 1:8, NLT).

Jesus, you are awesome and amazing, and you've proven yourself to
me again and again. I want to tell the world about the things I've
witnessed you do and the important truths you've taught me. I want
others to know that abundant life and hope are found in you and
only you. But it's not always easy. Sometimes my fears and insecurities
keep me from getting the words out. Other times the words come out
and don't make sense.

When I work in tandem with the Holy Spirit, powerful things happen.
My mouth moves, and messages come out that I didn't even have in
my head. And those messages impact lives. It's so much fun! Thank
you for giving me stories to tell and for the power to get them said.

What has been your experience with telling people
about Jesus?

HIS PLANS FOR MY LIFE

The LORD will work out his plans for my life—
for your faithful love, O LORD, endures forever.
Don't abandon me, for you made me (Psalm 138:8, NLT).

Lord, sometimes I get stuck and it seems as if I'm going nowhere.
I get frustrated when I want to move forward and can't. At times I
feel as if you've abandoned me and left me to figure things out on
my own. But I can't trust my feelings, Lord. Feelings change and you
don't. You are always there.

When it appears the plans for my life have been put on hold, you just
want me to lean harder into you and to acknowledge you. You made
me and won't abandon me. Your faithful love endures forever. You
have great plans for my life.

What do you do when it seems as if God's plans for you are
going nowhere?

May 26

No Lack

The Lord is my Shepherd [to feed, guide, and shield me],
I shall not lack (Psalm 23:1, AMP).

Lord, you are my faithful shepherd. You feed me, guide me, and shield me. You also provide everything I need. A jar of peanut butter and a tent would suffice, but you liberally supply so much more. You delight in giving me good things.

Because you are wiser than I am, you don't allow me everything I want. You know that some of the things I desire would be harmful for me, and your number one concern is keeping me safe. Thank you for making sure I lack nothing physically or spiritually to become the person you want me to be.

How has your faithful shepherd supplied your needs?

May 27
GREEN PASTURES

He makes me lie down in [fresh, tender] green pastures; He leads me beside the still and restful waters (Psalm 23:2, AMP).

You want me to rest, Lord. You want me to rest. So you provide a place where I can do that. You don't lead me to a barren dessert. Instead you guide me to lush green pastures—a nice, comfortable spot—and you make me lie down. While I'm lying there, I can put all my cares and concerns aside.

After I spend time in your green pastures and drink from your still waters, I'm refreshed and have the energy to move forward with whatever you have for me to do. Thank you for your rest, Lord. Thank you for your rest.

Is it time for you to lie down and rest?

May 28

REFRESHMENT, RESTORATION, AND RIGHT PATHS

He refreshes and restores my life (my self); He leads me in the paths of righteousness [uprightness and right standing with Him—not for my earning it, but] for His name's sake (Psalm 23:3, AMP).

Lord, at times I feel tired and worn out, as if I have nothing more to offer. I'm tempted to find a dark cave and never come out. You know that when I'm exhausted, my judgment is affected, so you woo me to your green pastures and still waters. You refresh and restore my life. You lead me on the right paths—your paths—paths you have personally prepared for me, and it's all to bring honor to your name.

How has God refreshed and restored you?

May 29

COMFORT

Though I walk through the [deep, sunless] valley of the shadow of death, I will fear or dread no evil, for You are with me; Your rod [to protect] and Your staff [to guide], they comfort me
(Psalm 23:4, AMP).

As I walk through the dark valley, Lord, I have no reason to fear because you are with me. Sometimes you're in front of me leading the way. Other times you're behind me covering me with your shadow. When I don't think I can make it any further, you're beside me, holding me up with your strong arm wrapped tightly around me.

You don't leave me in the valley, Lord. You take me through it. Your grace is sufficient. Someday I'll be on the other side, and it'll be a glorious place.

What comfort do you receive knowing God is with you in the dark valley?

May 30
OVERFLOWING CUP

You prepare a table before me in the presence of my enemies.
You anoint my head with oil; my [brimming] cup runs over
(Psalm 23:5, AMP).

You welcome me to your table, Lord. When I'm dining with you and delighting in your presence, I'm not hurried, agitated, or disturbed. I enjoy your feast while the enemies watch. They can't bother me because my focus is on you, and I'm at perfect peace.

I'm your honored guest, Lord. You meet my needs, you give me rest, you refresh me, you protect me, you strengthen me, you fellowship with me, and you anoint my head with oil. My cup overflows with joy.

What do you enjoy most about sitting at God's table?

May 31
GOODNESS, MERCY, AND LOVE

Surely or *only goodness, mercy,* and *unfailing love shall follow me all the days of my life, and through the length of my days the house of the Lord [and His presence] shall be my dwelling place*
(Psalm 23:6, AMP).

Lord, life isn't always easy. I face dark valleys, enemies, danger, exhaustion, paths that lead me astray, and many trying circumstances. But when I turn around, I see your goodness, mercy, and love pursuing me. They're always there—regardless of what's ahead—and they've never failed me.

Because I'm assured of your presence, I can face today and tomorrow with joy, peace, and hope. I look forward to dwelling in the peace and joy of your presence forever.

In what ways and in what situations have you experienced God's goodness, mercy, and love?

June

He guards the lives of his faithful ones

and delivers them from the hand of the wicked.

Light shines on the righteous

and joy on the upright in heart.

Rejoice in the LORD, you who are righteous,

and praise his holy name.

PSALM 97:10-12, NIV

June 1

UNFAILING LOVE

For his unfailing love toward those who fear him
is as great as the height of the heavens above the earth.
He has removed our sins as far from us
as the east is from the west (Psalm 103:11-12, NLT).

God, my heart has a hard time containing my love for you, yet the universe—the entire universe you made—can't contain the love you have for me. Your overwhelming love is unfailing and unchanging. It greets me in the morning when I awaken. It's there when I go to bed at night. And it's with me while I'm sleeping. Whether I'm facing hardships or celebrating victories, your love is there. I can't outrun it. I can't deny it.

Because of your great love, you remove my sins as far as the east is from the west. Because of your great love, you sent Jesus to carry them there. I praise you, God, for your love!

How would you describe God's unfailing love?

June 2

UPRIGHT AND JUST

"He is the Rock, his works are perfect,
and all his ways are just.
A faithful God who does no wrong,
upright and just is he" (Deuteronomy 32:4, NIV).

God, you are my rock—unshakable and unmovable—my firm foundation and support. Everything you do is perfect; you never mess up or make bad decisions. All your ways are guided by truth. I can trust you because you are a faithful God who does no wrong. You are upright and just. I'm thankful to be in your good and capable hands.

In what ways is God your rock?

June 3
SPRING RAIN

"Let us acknowledge the LORD;
let us press on to acknowledge him.
As surely as the sun rises,
he will appear;
he will come to us like the winter rains,
like the spring rains that water the earth" (Hosea 6:3, NIV).

My soul thirsts for you, Lord. I long to know you more and more.
As I seek you, you are faithful to appear—just as surely as the sun
rises each day. You come to me like the rains that water the earth.
The raindrops of your presence refresh, renew, and shower me with
the reality of who you are. They seep deep within me and connect
with my spirit in ways I can't express. With every drop, I'm reminded
of your love and goodness.

Thank you that the more I seek you, the more you'll soak me. Let it
rain, Lord. Let it rain. Open the floodgates of heaven and let it rain.
I want to absorb all you are and all you have for me.

How does God's rain refresh you?

June 4

No Teachers Needed

Whom did the Lord consult to enlighten him,
and who taught him the right way?
Who was it that taught him knowledge,
or showed him the path of understanding? (Isaiah 40:14, NIV)

Omniscient God, you existed before time began. From you—and only you—come knowledge, understanding, and wisdom. You created all things, you control all things, and you sustain all things. Why would I need you if you had to consult with me in order to run the world?

I'm thankful you want me to know you and that you reveal yourself to me in so many ways. You've promised if I seek you wholeheartedly and give you the honor you deserve, you will give me understanding, and I will gain knowledge of you. You will grant me wisdom. But no matter how much you give me, it won't match up to yours. My lack indicates my need for you, so I have no plans of applying for your job. You've got it covered and always will.

How does knowing of God's omniscience help you
to trust him more?

June 5

WHO IS HE?

Then He asked them, "Who do you think I am?"
Simon Peter answered, "The Christ, the Messiah,
the Son of the living God."
"God has blessed you, Simon, son of Jonah," Jesus said, "for my Father
in heaven has personally revealed this to you—this is not from any
human source" (Matthew 16:15-17, TLB).

"Who do *you* think I am?" What a question that is, Jesus!

Here's *who* I know you are: lover of my soul, giver of life, blesser of
each day, beautiful Savior, eternal God, Immanuel—God with us,
prince of peace, friend, blessed redeemer, living Word, almighty God,
alpha and omega, name above all names, truth, the way, light, good
shepherd, bread of life, the gate, the vine, pardon for sinners, healer,
author of salvation, hope for the nations, I AM.

Here's *what* I know you are: faithful, trustworthy,
compassionate, merciful, glorious, awesome, amazing,
indescribable, worthy to be praised, my song.

Jesus, I love you for who you are, I love you for what you are,
and I love you for all the inexpressible reasons in my heart.

Who do you think Jesus is?

June 6

PURE WORDS

The words and promises of the Lord are pure words, like silver refined in an earthen furnace, purified seven times over (Psalm 12:6, AMP).

Your words and promises are different from those of others, Lord. They're free from deception and falsehood. When you say you're going to do something, you do it. Your words and promises are pure.

You don't say things to manipulate others. You don't say things you'll regret. You don't say what itching ears want to hear. Your words and promises are pure.

They're words that encourage, comfort, teach, and guide. They're words that impact lives from generation to generation. Your words and promises are pure.

People can try to dispute them, but they ring true through the ages. The more they're tried, the more excellent they become. Your words and promises are pure.

Thank you, Lord, that your words and promises are pure. I can trust them and I can trust you.

How do you know God's words and promises are true?

June 7

HIS RIGHT HAND

"Your right hand, O LORD,
is glorious in power.
Your right hand, O LORD,
smashes the enemy.
In the greatness of your majesty,
you overthrow those who rise against you.
You unleash your blazing fury;
it consumes them like straw" (Exodus 15:6-7, NLT).

I marvel at your right hand, Lord. It's glorious in power. With it you smash the enemy and overthrow those who rise against you. Your right hand achieves awesome deeds and does mighty things. It brings victory. With your right hand you save, help, and deliver; you spread out the heavens. Eternal pleasures and righteousness are at your right hand, and that's where Jesus sits and intercedes on my behalf. Your right hand sustains me, upholds me, and holds me fast.

Nothing is a match for your majestic right hand, Lord. Thank you for stretching it out and using it for me. I'm grateful I'm not too small for your attention.

What comes to mind when you think of God's right hand?

June 8

Simple Prayers

"Don't recite the same prayer over and over as the heathen do, who think prayers are answered only by repeating them again and again. Remember, your Father knows exactly what you need even before you ask him!" (Matthew 6:7-8, TLB)

Father, I've heard many teachings and opinions about how to pray, but if I had to worry about using the proper formula or following a certain set of guidelines each time I approached you, I wouldn't come to you at all.

When I pray, I don't want to think about the technique. I come to you in childlike confidence because you're my Abba. I know you, I know how big you are, and I trust your love for me. Thank you for letting me talk to you honestly and without conditions. I want to believe in you and not the prayer.

What is your approach to prayer?

June 9

THE LORD IS GOD

You were shown these things so that you might know that the LORD is God; besides him there is no other (Deuteronomy 4:35, NIV).

Lord, you are God. Besides you there is no other. What god is there in heaven or on earth who can do the deeds and mighty works you do? You created man and put him on earth. You spoke from a burning bush. You parted the sea so people could walk across on dry ground. You've done countless things in former days and through today that prove you alone are God.

You've displayed your power in my own life again and again in amazing ways. Yet I forget, Lord. I know that you are God. I know there is no other. But sometimes I don't live as if I believe it. When uncomfortable situations come along, I forget. When I'm feeling weak and dwelling on my insufficiencies, I forget. And the reason I forget is that I take my eyes off of you. Help me keep my eyes on you and remember not to forget.

When have you forgotten that the Lord is God?

June 10

JESUS WEEPS

Jesus wept (John 11:35, NIV).

Jesus, you wept. That means I can, too. Thank you for
understanding my sorrow and sharing my grief.

How are you comforted in knowing that Jesus wept?

June 11

HE HEALS THE BROKENHEARTED

He heals the brokenhearted
and bandages their wounds (Psalm 147:3, NLT).

Lord, I feel as if my heart is so broken it will never heal. Yet even in my moments of profound grief and pain, I hear your gentle whisper reminding me that you will never fail or abandon me. I might not feel your presence, but you are here.

You are a man of sorrows, acquainted with deepest grief, and you understand how much I hurt. You heal the brokenhearted and bandage their wounds, and you will do that for me. The pain is temporary; your love for me is eternal.

What wounds do you need the Lord to bandage?

June 12
COMFORT AND ENCOURAGEMENT

What a wonderful God we have—he is the Father of our Lord Jesus
Christ, the source of every mercy, and the one who so wonderfully
comforts and strengthens us in our hardships and trials. And why does
he do this? So that when others are troubled, needing our sympathy
and encouragement, we can pass on to them this same help and
comfort God has given us. You can be sure that the more we undergo
sufferings for Christ, the more he will shower us with his comfort and
encouragement (2 Corinthians 1:3-5, TLB).

Lord, although I don't enjoy hardships or trials, I can honestly thank
you for allowing them in my life because of the benefits for me
and others. It's during the difficult times that my head knowledge
of you turns to reality in my heart. I come to know you and love
you in deeper, more intimate ways as you comfort, encourage, and
strengthen me.

You also repurpose my pain and give me the privilege of passing on
to others the same help and comfort you've given me. Thank you for
your perfect plan.

What benefits have you noticed in hardships or trials?

June 13

The Heavens Declare

The heavens declare the glory of God;
the skies proclaim the work of his hands (Psalm 19:1, NIV).

Magnificent Creator God, the heavens declare how amazing you are, and the skies testify to your breathtaking artistry! How can we escape the exquisite details of your solar system, and how can we overlook the display of splendor that greets us whenever we lift our eyes? The beauty and grandeur are far beyond our imagination and understanding.

Yet we silly humans think we can figure it out by spending billions of dollars and sending rockets, capsules, shuttles, and satellites into space. It's not going to happen, Lord! No one will comprehend the handiwork—or the love that put it in place—of a God who is limitless.

You and your works are glorious. You deserve all honor, worship, and praise.

How do the heavens speak to you about God?

June 14

BY HIS SPIRIT

"This is God's message to Zerubbabel: 'Not by might, nor by power, but by my Spirit, says the Lord Almighty—you will succeed because of my Spirit, though you are few and weak'" (Zechariah 4:6, TLB).

I'm feeling weak and inadequate right now, Lord. I wonder how I'm going to accomplish the great project you've called me to do. As I survey the enormity of the task before me and compare that to who I am, I'm ready to quit. But as I look to you for help, you remind me it's not by might, nor by power, but by your Spirit that I will succeed.

Thank you that I don't have to rely on myself. I look forward to a great outcome and to bragging on you in big ways for what you'll do in spite of me.

*When have you experienced success
in spite of your weakness?*

June 15

A Room Prepared

"There is more than enough room in my Father's home. If this were not so, would I have told you that I am going to prepare a place for you? When everything is ready, I will come and get you, so that you will always be with me where I am" (John 14:2-3, NLT).

Jesus, I love thinking about living forever with you in your Father's home. Thank you for preparing a place for me there. Thank you for providing the way for me to get there. Thank you for having enough room for me and for all the others who love you.

I expectantly await your return for me. In the meantime, I will delight in singing your praises here on earth so I'll be ready to do it throughout eternity.

How do you imagine life forever with Jesus in his Father's home?

June 16

ABBA, FATHER

Because we are his children, God has sent the Spirit of his Son into our hearts, prompting us to call out, "Abba, Father." Now you are no longer a slave but God's own child. And since you are his child, God has made you his heir (Galatians 4:6-7, NLT).

God, you're my Abba—my father, my daddy—and you want to make sure I know it! Thank you for sending the Spirit of your Son into my heart to tell me! Just being able to call you my Father fills me with joy, but you've also made me your heir, and I get to spend eternity with you! I'm overwhelmed with gratitude.

I want to bring you pleasure, Father. May my desires honor you, and may you delight in the way I delight in you. I love you and am privileged to be called your child.

How does it feel to be God's child?

June 17

MORE VALUABLE THAN BIRDS

"So my counsel is: Don't worry about things—food, drink, and clothes. For you already have life and a body—and they are far more important than what to eat and wear. Look at the birds! They don't worry about what to eat—they don't need to sow or reap or store up food—for your heavenly Father feeds them. And you are far more valuable to him than they are" (Matthew 6:25-26, TLB).

As I observe the brilliant red cardinals in the tree and the eastern goldfinch in the thistle, I'm in awe of your handiwork, Lord. You obviously value them because of the intricacy and beauty of their design. I listen to their melodious warbles and cheerful twitters and my spirit knows that they're singing praise songs to you. They're worry free and joyful in your care.

Lord, you value me much more than your remarkable birds. Why wouldn't you care for my every need? Thank you for this important reminder.

What do you learn about God's care from the birds?

June 18

WILDFLOWER BEAUTY

"Which of you by being anxious can add a single hour to his span of life? And why are you anxious about clothing? Consider the lilies of the field, how they grow: they neither toil nor spin, yet I tell you, even Solomon in all his glory was not arrayed like one of these"
(Matthew 6:27-29, ESV).

Lord, clothes don't make the person. You do. So why do I worry about how I look? Why do I get caught up in what others think is beautiful? It's so easy to fall into the "too" trap. I'm too fat. Too short. Too plain. Too blemished. Too ugly. I have too many excess hairs.

Remind me that the way you see me is most important. It doesn't matter how I'm dressed. My personal appearance doesn't matter. I'm one of your uniquely beautiful and highly valued flowers. And your bouquets are fabulous!

Which one of God's beautiful flowers do you most resemble?

June 19

GOD-PROVISIONS

"God clothes the grass in the field, which is alive today but tomorrow is thrown into the fire. So you can be even more sure that God will clothe you. Don't have so little faith! Don't worry and say, 'What will we eat?' or 'What will we drink?' or 'What will we wear?' The people who don't know God keep trying to get these things, and your Father in heaven knows you need them. Seek first God's kingdom and what God wants. Then all your other needs will be met as well"
(Matthew 6:30-33, NCV).

God, if I remember how you've proven yourself to me so many times in the past; and if I remember the countless ways you've provided for me; and if I remember that you have a perfect plan for my life, I won't worry about missing out. I will trust you to attend to my every need and to do what's best for me. Help me to steep my life in your reality today.

How has God attended to your needs in the past?

June 20
THINK ABOUT TODAY

"Don't worry about tomorrow, because tomorrow will have its own
worries. Each day has enough trouble of its own"
(Matthew 6:34, NCV).

Lord, sometimes I get so consumed with the cares and concerns—or
dreams—of tomorrow that I forget to think about today. I need to
remember that you have a purpose for me right here, right now.
Why else did you give me this day?

One experience today can teach me an important truth about who you
are. One hour in prayer today can draw me closer to you. One thing I
say or do today can cause an eternal difference in the life of my loved
one. One decision I make today can impact generations to come. One
today in your hands can change the course of the rest of my days.

Every today is an important thread in the beautiful tapestry you're
weaving of my life. Thank you for each today you give me, Lord.
May I use them all for your glory.

What's happening in your life today?

June 21

HE'S NOT WEAK

Moses said, "There are 600,000 men alone besides all the women and
children, and yet you promise them meat for a whole month!
If we butcher all our flocks and herds it won't be enough! We would
have to catch every fish in the ocean to fulfill your promise!"
Then the Lord said to Moses, "When did I become weak?
Now you shall see whether my word comes true or not!"
(Numbers 11:21-23, TLB)

Lord, the situation seems ludicrous! How is it possible that you
had to ask Moses, "When did I become weak?" Hadn't he just
experienced the burning bush, the ten plagues, the amazing rescue
from the Egyptians, the parting of the Red Sea, your obvious
presence with him in the pillar of cloud, the provision of manna,
and many other great deeds?

But then, how is it possible that you have to ask me the same question?
That's ludicrous, too. Forgive me for my wavering trust in you.

How would you answer God's question: "When did I become
weak?"

June 22

THE STARS

God said, "Let lights appear in the sky to separate the day from the
night. Let them be signs to mark the seasons, days, and years. Let
these lights in the sky shine down on the earth." And that is what
happened. God made two great lights—the larger one to govern the
day, and the smaller one to govern the night. He also made the stars
(Genesis 1:14-16, NLT).

God, I'm astounded at the use of five simple words to describe your
complex universe: "He also made the stars." It's as if it was no big
deal for you—and it really wasn't. Of far greater importance to you is
having a relationship with your people.

Thank you for wanting communion with me. Thank you for making it
possible for me to share intimacy with the God who made the stars.
I'm in awe of your ways.

How do you feel knowing that the God who made the stars
wants a relationship with you?

June 23

MANY OTHER THINGS

Jesus did many other things as well. If every one of them were written down, I suppose that even the whole world would not have room for the books that would be written (John 21:25, NIV).

Jesus, I feel the same way about the things you've done in my life. If every one of them were written down, I suppose that even the whole world would not have room for the books that would be written. Every day you shower me with reminders of your goodness and love.

Thank you for the way you pour out your blessings and abundance. Thank you for your involvement and impact on my life. Thank you for giving me words to express my gratitude for you. And thank you that when I run out of words, you can read the song on my heart. May I never lose the sense of wonder and appreciation I have for you, Lord! You are worthy to be honored and praised forever and ever.

If you were to write down all the things Jesus has done for you, what would be the first ten on your list?

June 24

LIVING GOD

"Of what value is an idol carved by a craftsman?
Or an image that teaches lies?
For the one who makes it trusts in his own creation;
he makes idols that cannot speak.
Woe to him who says to wood, 'Come to life!'
Or to lifeless stone, 'Wake up!'
Can it give guidance?
It is covered with gold and silver;
there is no breath in it."
The LORD is in his holy temple;
let all the earth be silent before him" (Habakkuk 2:18-20, NIV).

Some things make no sense to me, Lord, and this is one of them. Why would people choose to worship an idol of their own creation when they could worship you, the creator of all things? What value is an object that can be thrown into a backpack and carried on a person's shoulders? Wouldn't it be better to worship a God who can't be contained?

How can a breathless, speechless idol compare to the living God who speaks and the whole earth listens? It's no contest, Lord. And it's a good reminder. Help me to keep my life free from idols.

Have you ever worshiped anything other than God?

June 25

ALIVE AND POWERFUL WORD

The word of God is alive and powerful. It is sharper than the sharpest two-edged sword, cutting between soul and spirit, between joint and marrow. It exposes our innermost thoughts and desires (Hebrews 4:12, NLT).

I praise you, loving Father, for being a relational God and for communicating with me in intimate ways. As our spirits connect on the pages of Scripture, I'm aware of how well you know me and what I need to hear. Although they were written many years ago to a different people in a different place, your words impact me deeply right now. They encourage, convict, challenge, and guide.

Your words are like raindrops, Lord. They water the weary, parched places of my soul and saturate my mind with truth. They give me life and vitality. They help me grow in grace and knowledge of you. And they strengthen my heart with reminders of your power, presence, and purpose. Your words are alive, effective, fresh, and new for each day. I'm grateful for the gift of your words, Lord. They've transformed my life.

In what ways have you experienced God's Word being alive and powerful?

June 26

ADOPTED INTO THE FAMILY

His unchanging plan has always been to adopt us into his own family
by sending Jesus Christ to die for us. And he did this because he
wanted to! Now all praise to God for his wonderful kindness to us
and his favor that he has poured out upon us because we belong
to his dearly loved Son (Ephesians 1:5-6, TLB).

Years ago you made plans to adopt me into your own family, and
you took pleasure in working out the details. You prepared a room for
me in your spacious house, set aside new clothes for me to wear, and
dreamed of the things we'd do together in the future.

When the eagerly anticipated day finally arrived—the day the papers
were signed—you celebrated by throwing a party for me complete with
lavish gifts. Father God, how can I ever thank you enough for your
extravagant love? I adore you.

What benefits do you enjoy as a member of God's family?

June 27

In Him

In him we live and move and have our being (Acts 17:28a, NIV).

God, you fill the atmosphere. There's no getting away from you.
I live in you. I move in you. I have my being in you.

You give me breath. You infuse me with life. You determine my
purpose. You nourish and sustain me. You energize me. You satisfy my
soul. You lift me up. You help me soar. You put a song in my heart.

I wouldn't exist without you. I couldn't survive without you.
I don't even want to try. May my living and moving and being
bring you great joy.

*What does it mean to you to live and move
and have your being in him?*

June 28

HOLY SPIRIT HELP

The Holy Spirit helps us in our weakness. For example, we don't know what God wants us to pray for. But the Holy Spirit prays for us with groanings that cannot be expressed in words. And the Father who knows all hearts knows what the Spirit is saying, for the Spirit pleads for us believers in harmony with God's own will
(Romans 8:26-27, NLT).

Father, there's so much on my heart that's inexpressible. Burdens lay deep within me, and my emotions indicate a heaviness there, yet I'm unaware of the root cause. I'm grateful that you don't expect me to know how to pray in those situations! You've given me the Holy Spirit, who helps me in my weakness.

When I don't know how to communicate my feelings, the Spirit prays for me with groanings that only you can understand. You interpret the language of my heart and you minister to me in harmony with your will. Thank you for the comfort you provide.

What conversation is the Spirit having with the Father on your behalf right now?

June 29

WELL-WATERED GARDEN

"The LORD will guide you always;
he will satisfy your needs in a sun-scorched land
and will strengthen your frame.
You will be like a well-watered garden,
like a spring whose waters never fail" (Isaiah 58:11, NIV).

God, I'm living in a sun-scorched land, and all around me people are affected by the intense heat. Their hope has shriveled and their spirits are parched. I want to lead them to the oasis, but I'm weary and in need of refreshment myself.

So right now I come to you to drink deeply from the source of living water. I trust you to strengthen and sustain me and to turn me into a fruitful garden in the midst of the vast desert. I trust that I'll be like a spring whose waters never fail. Thank you that as I help satisfy the needs of others, you are faithful to satisfy mine.

How is God using you in a sun-scorched land
to satisfy the needs of others?

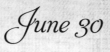

June 30

OVERWHELMED WITH JOY

I am overwhelmed with joy in the LORD my God!
For he has dressed me with the clothing of salvation
and draped me in a robe of righteousness.
I am like a bridegroom dressed for his wedding
or a bride with her jewels (Isaiah 61:10, NLT).

I love my new clothes, God! Thanks for providing them for me. I know they came at a great price and I want to wear them well. My old wardrobe was repugnant and didn't flatter me at all. But the beautiful white tailor-made robe you wrapped around me is flawless! As I wear it, I notice a fragrance wafting through the air, and the heavenly aroma reminds me of you.

I'm overwhelmed with joy that you have dressed me with the clothing of salvation, Lord! May you look upon me and smile.

How do you look in your new clothes?

July

He has saved us and called us to a
holy life—not because of anything we
have done but because of his own purpose
and grace. This grace was given us in
Christ Jesus before the beginning of time.

2 TIMOTHY 1:9, NIV

July 1

ADVANTAGES IN SUFFERING

My suffering was good for me,
for it taught me to pay attention to your decrees (Psalm 119:71, NLT).

Yes, Lord, my suffering is good for me. It's not fun, but I can see how you use it for my benefit and your glory. It's made me the person I am today and taught me about what's most important in life.

Through suffering, I learned the joy of your presence, the richness of your Word, and the value of friends. I also learned about your all-sufficient and amazing grace. Through suffering, I became more caring, more loving, more compassionate, more empathetic, and more sensitive to other's needs.

Through suffering, I've gained a deeper faith, a closer relationship with you, a stronger spirit, the qualifications to help others, and wisdom. Thank you for teaching me that even in suffering you have purpose.

What have you learned through suffering?

July 2
KNOW THE HOPE

I pray that the eyes of your heart may be enlightened in order that you may know the hope to which he has called you, the riches of his glorious inheritance in his holy people (Ephesians 1:18, NIV).

Open the eyes of my heart, Lord. I want to see you and know you in more intimate ways. It's in my growing closer to you that you reveal the certainty of your glorious hope.

Hope is only as good as its object, and I praise you for being a God who is reliable and trustworthy. Your word is always true. You have a purpose and plan for me today, and you have a bright future awaiting me—an eternity with you. My hope rests in you.

How is God revealing his hope to you today?

July 3
GOD'S STRANGE WAYS

When the trumpets sounded, the army shouted, and at the sound
of the trumpet, when the men gave a loud shout, the wall collapsed;
so everyone charged straight in, and they took the city
(Joshua 6:20, NIV).

God, I smile as I think about your methods. They make no sense to me, yet when you give instructions—no matter how strange—and people obey, remarkable things happen. That way you get the glory and not someone else.

It's a lesson I need to remember when you ask me to do things that seem beyond reason. My job is to trust and obey, then get out of the way. When I do that, you show up and show off every time. I love the way you work, Lord! Thank you for including me in your unusual plans.

When has God asked you to do something unusual?

July 4
INDEPENDENCE DAY

*He is so rich in kindness and grace that he purchased our freedom
with the blood of his Son and forgave our sins. He has showered his
kindness on us, along with all wisdom and understanding
(Ephesians 1:7-8, NLT).*

Loving God, independence is freedom from the control of others, yet I
celebrate my independence day as the day I let Jesus take control of
my life. When I did that, I was freed from the power of sin and death.

I realize that true freedom comes at a great price, Lord. May I never
take lightly the high cost Jesus paid for mine. Thank you for your
kindness and grace.

How do you celebrate your Independence Day?

July 5

SUN AND SHIELD

The LORD God is a sun and shield;
the LORD bestows favor and honor;
No good thing does he withhold
from those whose walk is blameless.
LORD Almighty,
blessed is the one who trusts in you
(Psalm 84:11-12, NIV).

Lord Almighty, I trust in you and I'm blessed by your abundant goodness. Just as the sun appears every day, you are reliable. I can depend on you because you are the same yesterday, today, and forever. As I soak in your rays of light, you warm my heart, enlighten my mind, refresh my soul, and provide the energy I need to carry on.

Many things threaten me daily, but I'm safe with you as my shield. You're always on duty, and nothing gets past you without your permission. Thank you for bestowing your favor and honor on me. May I glorify you in all I do, and may you look down on me and smile.

How does God act as your sun and shield?

July 6
KING OF NATIONS

LORD, there is no one like you!
For you are great, and your name is full of power.
Who would not fear you, O King of nations?
That title belongs to you alone!
Among all the wise people of the earth
and in all the kingdoms of the world,
there is no one like you (Jeremiah 10:6-7, NLT).

Lord, your name is great and greatly to be praised! You deserve all honor, for there is no one like you. No king or president or leader even comes close in comparison. You are superior in wisdom, superior in power, and you alone hold the title "King of Nations."

Nothing happens in this world without your awareness, nor does anything catch you by surprise, Lord. You are still on the throne. You haven't left it and never will.

I may not understand your ways, but I do know that you are in control and you are sovereign. I have no need for worry or concern because you are in charge. Thank you for being my faithful, trustworthy, almighty God.

How are you helped knowing that God is
the King of nations?

July 7

PRESENT IN DEEP WATERS

When you go through deep waters and great trouble, I will be with
you. When you go through rivers of difficulty, you will not drown!
(Isaiah 43:2a, TLB)

Lord, you didn't promise to keep your loved ones from trouble; you
promised that when they went through deep waters you would be
with them and that they wouldn't drown. I know you're fully able
to prevent rivers of difficulty; therefore, you must have a purpose in
allowing us to go through them. Could it be so we would know you
better? Could it be that we might learn to trust you more?

Whatever the reason, I'm thankful I can count on you to keep
me afloat. I'm comforted in knowing you are with me through all
I experience, and I'm blessed by your love.

What deep waters will you thank God for today?

July 8

IN THE FIRE

When you walk through the fire of oppression, you will not be burned up—the flames will not consume you (Isaiah 43:2b, TLB).

First rivers of difficulty and now the fire of oppression. Wow, Lord, I'm not excited about either! But you knew I would go through both and you made sure I had your promise that I would be okay.

Thank you for being my safe place. Thank you for your grace that carries me through the rivers and fires. And thank you for your comforting, loving, and compassionate presence in my life. May you be glorified in what happens in me and through me as I face the fires and rivers with you.

How can God use the fires and rivers in your life for good?

July 9

IN THE FURNACE

Then King Nebuchadnezzar leaped to his feet in amazement and asked his advisers, "Weren't there three men that we tied up and threw into the fire?" They replied, "Certainly, Your Majesty."

He said, "Look! I see four men walking around in the fire, unbound and unharmed, and the fourth looks like a son of the gods."

Nebuchadnezzar then approached the opening of the blazing furnace and shouted, "Shadrach, Meshach and Abednego, servants of the Most High God, come out! Come here!"

So Shadrach, Meshach and Abednego came out of the fire, and the satraps, prefects, governors and royal advisers crowded around them. They saw that the fire had not harmed their bodies, nor was a hair of their heads singed; their robes were not scorched, and there was no smell of fire on them.

Then Nebuchadnezzar said, "Praise be to the God of Shadrach, Meshach and Abednego, who has sent his angel and rescued his servants!" (Daniel 3:24-28, NIV)

God, all praise goes to you for the way you protect and rescue your servants! As I trust in you, you will take care of me.

How does this encourage you?

July 10

FRIENDSHIP WITH GOD

The LORD would speak to Moses face to face, as one speaks to a friend
(Exodus 33:11, NIV).

Lord, I'm grateful that I can enjoy the same kind of personal
relationship with you that Moses had. Through Jesus, I'm able to
approach you not just as my heavenly Father or the God of the
universe, but also as my friend. I can come to you at any time and
know you will be ready to hear from me.

Whether I'm walking, driving, working, or relaxing—whatever I'm
doing—you meet me where I am. You welcome my honest thoughts,
my deep conversations, my questions, my praise reports, and my
simple chitchat about my day-to-day happenings. I'm delighted
that you choose to reveal your heart and thoughts to me as well.
I treasure your love and friendship, Lord God. Thank you for the
intimacy we share.

In what ways do you enjoy friendship with God?

July 11

He Will Do It

"What I have said, that I will bring about;
what I have planned, that I will do" (Isaiah 46:11, NIV).

God, your word is truth. If you say you're going to do something, it will happen. There's no question about it. You will do what you have planned. Period. But what you didn't say is in what timeframe. Your sense of timing and mine are completely different.

Help me to trust your schedule for the matters of my life. You have the big picture, and you know what you're doing. May I wait on you with joy.

How is God's sense of timing in his plans different than yours?

July 12

CHRIST'S LOVE

*Can anything ever separate us from Christ's love? Does it mean he
no longer loves us if we have trouble or calamity, or are persecuted,
or hungry, or destitute, or in danger, or threatened with death? No,
despite all these things, overwhelming victory is ours through Christ,
who loved us (Romans 8:35-37, NLT).*

Lord, as I get to know you in closer, more intimate ways, I have
a deeper understanding of your character and your heart for
me. You love me unconditionally. Nothing can change that. Not
circumstances. Not hardships. Not suffering. Not debt. Not drought.

You are good, and you want to bless me and help me. Because I
know this to be true, I can see how you use the tribulations and
calamities in my life for me instead of against me. You've given
me access to your overcoming love, grace, and power; therefore,
overwhelming victory is mine! Thank you for giving me unshakable
assurance of your love.

How does trouble or calamity affect your love for God?

July 13

ALL-SEEING EYES

He knows about everyone, everywhere. Everything about us is bare
and wide open to the all-seeing eyes of our living God; nothing can
be hidden from him to whom we must explain all that we have done
(Hebrews 4:13, TLB).

God, may I be ever mindful of your all-seeing eyes. I'm comforted in
knowing that you see my heartaches and the things I'm concerned
about, and you care. But you also notice things about me I don't want
to face. I can't hide my sins, no matter how hard I try. Everything
about me is bare and wide open to you.

Lord, I ask that you reveal those things to me and help me to
deal with them according to your Word. I want to be the person
you want me to be.

What do God's all-seeing eyes notice about you?

July 14

BEYOND UNDERSTANDING

I will praise you, LORD, among the nations;
I will sing of you among the peoples.
For great is your love, reaching to the heavens;
your faithfulness reaches to the skies (Psalm 57:9-10, NIV).

Lord, I praise you because you are outside the parameters of my understanding. I can't see the end of your love and faithfulness. It reaches beyond this world. I can't grasp the magnitude of your greatness and grandeur. It's never-ending. I can't comprehend why you would care about me. It's a mystery.

I can't imagine what my life would be like without a relationship with you. I'm thankful that I don't have to. You are the most high God, the all-surpassing God, the God I love and adore.
What a privilege it is to serve you.

How will you praise the most high God today?

July 15
DELIVERANCE

Moses answered the people, "Do not be afraid. Stand firm and you will see the deliverance the LORD will bring you today. The Egyptians you see today you will never see again. The LORD will fight for you; you need only to be still" (Exodus 14:13-14, NIV).

Lord, I often find myself in a predicament where there seems no way out. It's during those times you want me to remember the instructions Moses gave the Israelites years ago: "Don't be afraid. Stand firm. Be still. See the deliverance."

It sounds so simple, Lord, but it's not. Sometimes while I'm waiting for you to rescue me, my faith wavers. If it doesn't happen in my expected timeframe, I start to doubt your promises. The enemy taunts me with lies that cause me to question your ability and love for me.

When that happens, Lord, help me to remember truth. Help me to have unshakable trust in your purposes and plans. Help me to be strong and courageous. And help me to praise you in advance for the deliverance I will see.

In what circumstances are you waiting and watching for God's deliverance?

July 16

EVERYTHING BEAUTIFUL

He has made everything beautiful in its time (Ecclesiastes 3:11, NIV).

You're creating a masterpiece with my life, Lord. I can't see the scope of your beautiful design because I'm right in the middle of it, but I trust that you know the plan from beginning to end. You have appointed my times and seasons—the good and the not-so-good—and knowing that you're in control gives me hope.

You have me right where you want me to be, and the finished product will be a fabulous work of art in your hands.

What beautiful work have you experienced God do in your life or a friend's life?

July 17

HE HIDES ME

The one thing I ask of the LORD—
the thing I seek most—
is to live in the house of the LORD all the days of my life,
delighting in the LORD's perfections
and meditating in his Temple.
For he will conceal me there when troubles come;
he will hide me in his sanctuary.
He will place me out of reach on a high rock.
Then I will hold my head high
above my enemies who surround me.
At his sanctuary I will offer sacrifices with shouts of joy,
singing and praising the LORD with music (Psalm 27:4-6, NLT).

Lord, you are my sanctuary, my rock, my secret place. How I praise you
for hiding me in your presence! As I meditate on you and delight in
your perfections, the burdens, troubles, chaos, disappointments and
discouragement—and all the things that chase me down—are quieted.

I'm able to hold my head high in your protective care. I love you, Lord,
and desire to dwell in your house all the days of my life. In you is
where I find my rest.

How does God hide you?

July 18

LORD OF HEAVEN AND EARTH

The God who made the world and everything in it is the Lord of
heaven and earth and does not live in temples built by human hands.
And he is not served by human hands, as if he needed anything.
Rather, he himself gives everyone life and breath and everything else
(Acts 17:24-25, NIV).

Lord of heaven and earth, I praise you because you are the everlasting-to-everlasting God. You were God before time began and you will be God throughout eternity. You're not a God created by human hands, nor are you contained by human structures. Instead, your hands made the heavens, the earth, and everything in them.

Everything that has life and breath has its needs met by you. You aren't dependent on anyone or anything, but you delight in those who want to serve you. I worship you, God. You are worthy of all honor and praise. May you be glorified in my devotion to you.

For what will you praise the Lord of heaven and earth today?

July 19
GIVER OF STRENGTH

I can do everything God asks me to with the help of Christ who gives me the strength and power (Philippians 4:13, TLB).

God, the Apostle Paul said that it didn't matter if he was rich or poor, hungry or well-fed, healthy or weak. Regardless of the circumstances he faced—and many of them were harsh—he was content. That was possible only through his dependence on you! You gave him strength and power to do the things you wanted him to do. And his life still impacts people in huge ways today.

Thank you for making that same strength and power available for me. When I'm weak, exhausted, and not up to the challenge of the things before me, I can count on you. You will sustain me when life seems unsustainable. I can do everything you ask me to do with the help you give me through Christ. May my life glorify you for years to come.

In what situations have you relied on the help of Christ's strength and power?"

July 20

Broke the Yoke

"I will walk among you; I will be your God, and you will be my people. I am the LORD your God, who brought you out of the land of Egypt so you would no longer be their slaves. I broke the yoke of slavery from your neck so you can walk with your heads held high"
(Leviticus 26:12-13, NLT).

Father God, as I think about these promises you gave the Israelites many years ago, I'm thankful that you are my God and that you walk with me daily. Your great love made possible my release from sin's yoke of slavery.

Because of Jesus' death and resurrection—and my choice to trust in him—I'm forgiven, free, and fully alive! I can walk with my head held high knowing whose I am, how loved I am, and with the assurance of a bright future with you. I'm blessed to be your child.

How does this speak to you?

July 21
HIS WORD

"The rain and snow come down from the heavens
and stay on the ground to water the earth.
They cause the grain to grow,
producing seed for the farmer
and bread for the hungry.
It is the same with my word.
I send it out, and it always produces fruit.
It will accomplish all I want it to,
and it will prosper everywhere I send it" (Isaiah 55:10-11, NLT).

Lord, I thank you for your powerful, productive, and purposeful Word. It's a gift that keeps on giving.

As vegetation relies on the moisture you send for nourishment, your Word is nutrition for my soul. When I allow it to descend on me and saturate my mind and heart, I grow in strong, healthy, and fruitful ways. May your Word dwell in me richly and may it accomplish your purposes for my life.

What fruit has God's Word produced in you?

July 22

MOURNING AND JOY

You have turned my mourning into joyful dancing.
You have taken away my clothes of mourning and
clothed me with joy,
that I might sing praises to you and not be silent.
O Lord my God, I will give you thanks forever! (Psalm 30:11-12, NLT)

God, thank you that my grief is not insignificant to you. Thank you for ministering to me in my sorrow. Thank you for reminding me that my mourning won't last forever. Thank you for working all things together for good. Thank you for making all things beautiful in your time. Thank you for specializing in transformation and hope. Thank you for giving me new clothes to replace my old ones.

Thank you for teaching me the dance steps to joy. I will sing praises to you and not be silent. I will give you thanks forever!

How is it possible for God to turn mourning
into joyful dancing?

July 23
THE GREATER SPIRIT

You belong to God, my dear children. You have already won a victory over those people, because the Spirit who lives in you is greater than the spirit who lives in the world (1 John 4:4, NLT).

Lord, this world is home to a powerful evil spirit—one that celebrates terrorism, violence, temptation, deception, agony, chaos, heartache, and hopelessness—and from all appearances, he's having great success. Thank you for not leaving me alone to fend for myself!

The evil one prowls around like a roaring lion looking for someone to devour. His voice is loud and he tells a convincing story, but he's a toothless wimp compared to the Spirit of truth within me. The adversary doesn't like it when I bombard him with reality. He doesn't like it when I call him the defeated one. He doesn't like it when I bring up the name of Jesus.

I praise you, Lord, for the victory that is mine! I praise you for your incomparably great power! I praise you for truth!
May it always be before me.

Who is greater in your life—the spirit of the world or the Spirit within you?

July 24

ETERNAL, IMMORTAL, INVISIBLE

Now to the King eternal, immortal, invisible, the only God,
be honor and glory for ever and ever. Amen (1 Timothy 1:17, NIV).

Most high God, the living God, the only God—I exalt your name. You deserve all honor and glory for ever and ever, for you are infinitely greater than any created god or being.

You are the King of nations and King of kings, supreme in power and authority. Your kingdom is unshakable and your reign is everlasting. You are the alpha and omega, the beginning and the end.

I praise you because you are different than man. You don't change your mind or change your plan. You are immortal and incorruptible, and you will be celebrated throughout all time.

Invisible God, your splendor and majesty fill the heavens and earth. One day I will see you face to face, and it will be my honor to bow before you. Holy Lord, God Almighty, you are worthy to be worshiped and adored today, tomorrow, and to the end of the age.

How will you worship God today?

July 25
GOD'S REMINDER

He is able to save completely all who come to God through him.
Since he will live forever, he will always be there to remind God that
he has paid for their sins with his blood (Hebrews 7:25, TLB).

Jesus, I don't know what to say, but thank you.

What is your response to Jesus?

July 26
EVERYTHING IS POSSIBLE

Jesus looked at them intently and said, "Humanly speaking, it is impossible. But with God everything is possible"
(Matthew 19:26, NLT).

God, humanly speaking, my life and the world around me are filled with impossible things, but I casually accept them as normal.

How is it possible that the sun doesn't fall from the sky? How is it possible that the dead things of winter come back to life in the spring? How is it possible that I have a beating heart? How is it possible that intricately designed babies develop from a tiny seed? How is it possible that someone would give up his only Son to die for the entire world?

Forgive me for not acknowledging your work, God. Forgive me for not being more in awe of you. Forgive me for not being more grateful. Forgive me for not recognizing the extent of your love for me. May I never lose the wonder of the many impossible things you do. They all point to a wonderful, powerful, caring God.

As you open your eyes to your life and the world around you, what impossible things do you notice?

July 27
PEACE

"Peace I leave with you; my peace I give you. I do not give to you as the world gives. Do not let your hearts be troubled and do not be afraid" (John 14:27, NIV).

Jesus, thank you for your wonderful gift of peace. It's not like the so-called peace the world gives, which is based on resources or lack of trouble and doesn't last. Your peace is available in spite of perfect circumstances. It comes from living in relationship with you.

When I focus on you and praise you in the midst of whatever I'm going through, and when I live in the center of your will, you bring a sense of tranquility to my soul. The anxieties, unknowns, and what ifs that would otherwise overwhelm me are stilled.

Would you please fill me with your peace that surpasses all understanding so that it's obvious to those around me, Lord? In this world that's filled with confusion and fear, your enduring peace is desperately needed. I want to shine the light on you and introduce others to the source.

What is your experience with the peace that Jesus gives?

July 28

THE PERFECT FATHER

Even if my father and mother abandon me,
the LORD will hold me close (Psalm 27:10, NLT).

Heavenly Father, I praise you for being the perfect Father. I praise you for loving me without conditions. I praise you for being kind and forgiving. I praise you for your goodness and generosity. I praise you for your wisdom and advice that's always right. I praise you for your unparalleled strength. I praise you for being trustworthy and faithful. I praise you for your promise that you will never leave me or forsake me.

Even if my earthly father and mother abandon me, or even if they fail me, or even if they disappoint me, you never will. You will hold me close. There's no better place to be than in your loving, caring arms.

How does the heavenly Father compare
to your earthly parents?

July 29

HE KNOWS AND SEES

You know when I sit down or stand up.
You know my thoughts even when I'm far away.
You see me when I travel
and when I rest at home.
You know everything I do.
You know what I am going to say
even before I say it, Lord (Psalm 139:2-4, NLT).

Lord, wherever I am and whatever I'm doing, you see me. When I'm crying in the corner of my bedroom over the choices a loved one is making, you see me. When I'm standing before a large audience to give a presentation, you see me. When I'm driving through a dangerous part of town, you see me.

Not only do you see everything I do, but you know everything about me as well. You know my heartaches. You know my apprehensions. You know my fears and doubts. You even know what I'm going to say before I say it. Nothing gets past you, Lord. Because you're fully aware of all things in my life at all times, you know just what I need and when I need it. For that I praise you.

How does God's all-seeing, all-knowing presence comfort you?

July 30

No Excuses

Moses pleaded with the Lord, "O Lord, I'm not very good with words. I never have been, and I'm not now, even though you have spoken to me. I get tongue-tied, and my words get tangled."

Then the Lord asked Moses, "Who makes a person's mouth? Who decides whether people speak or do not speak, hear or do not hear, see or do not see? Is it not I, the Lord? Now go! I will be with you as you speak, and I will instruct you in what to say"

(Exodus 4:10-12, NLT).

O Lord, I've had many Moses moments, and I've used all the same excuses he did. But I shouldn't because I know you. I know you're with me. I know you're a big God. I know when you give assignments, you provide the way to carry them out. So God, help me in those moments to steer my attention away from my inadequacies to you and your sufficiency. Instead of coming up with reasons why I can't do something, may I please you by trusting you and saying, "Whatever, Lord." I want to serve you well.

What excuses have you given God?

July 31
GOOD GIFTS

"Which of you, if your son asks for bread, will give him a stone? Or if he asks for a fish, will give him a snake? If you, then, though you are evil, know how to give good gifts to your children, how much more will your Father in heaven give good gifts to those who ask him!"
(Matthew 7:9-11, NIV)

Father, the better I understand the depth of your love for me, the more confident I am in coming to you with my requests. You don't laugh at me or turn me away; instead, you welcome me with open arms. As I delight in you, you delight in giving me the desires of my heart—some I didn't even know I had! You are so gracious to me, God.

I envision your smile as you shower me with generosity. I don't deserve any of your gifts, yet you pour them out in lavish ways because that's the nature of who you are. You are a good and kind-hearted God. Thank you for your good gifts. May my enjoyment of them bring you pleasure.

What good gifts have you enjoyed from God's hand?

August

God will generously provide all you need.

Then you will always have everything you need

and plenty left over to share with others.

2 CORINTHIANS 9:8, NLT

August 1
No Condemnation

There is no condemnation for those who belong to Christ Jesus
(Romans 8:1, NLT).

Lord, I want to live for you and serve you well, but I goof up
constantly. I make mistakes. I fail. I sin. I disappoint myself and often
feel as if I've disappointed you. I'm grateful that because I belong to
Jesus I don't have to live in fear of condemnation. At times, though, I
struggle to fully grasp that incredible promise.

I'm hard on myself. My own judgmental thoughts turn against me and
cause me to lose sight of your forgiveness. But if you—the righteous
God—don't condemn me, then why should I condemn myself? That
would be like saying I'm better than you, and it would allow Satan
the victory. I don't want that, Lord. Help me to remember that those
thoughts are not from you.

Thank you for your goodness and kindness. Thank you for your
grace. And thank you that the blood of Christ was sufficient for my
forgiveness yesterday, today, and tomorrow. I love you, Lord!

When have you had trouble believing this promise?

August 2
GOD'S WORD STANDS

"The grass withers and the flowers fade
beneath the breath of the LORD.
And so it is with people.
The grass withers and the flowers fade,
but the word of our God stands forever" (Isaiah 40:7-8, NLT).

Lord, people in our lives come and go. Friendships fail. Our bodies waste away. The economy is constantly in flux. World affairs deteriorate. Our beloved possessions fall apart. The grass withers and the flowers fade. We can't count on anyone or anything to be unchanging or infallible—except for you and your Word.

Your Word is constant through the ages. It created life and transforms people. It gives hope, instruction, challenge, encouragement, and direction, and it's just as good today as it was in the beginning. I praise you for your excellent, unfailing, powerful, and enduring Word! Your Word stands forever. May I stand on it to guide my life.

What does God's Word mean to you?

August 3

God Acts on My Behalf

Since ancient times no one has heard,
no ear has perceived,
no eye has seen any God besides you,
who acts on behalf of those who wait for him (Isaiah 64:4, NIV).

God, I get restless waiting for a cup of coffee to brew, so when it comes to waiting for the new thing in my life, or for a promise to be fulfilled, the holding period can be hard to endure.

I'm learning that you have a purpose in the waiting. The Bible includes many instances of people who held on for years before their awaited time came, and I see how you were at work behind the scenes shaping their characters, teaching them about you, and uniquely equipping them for the important jobs you had in store for them.

Help me learn to embrace the waiting process in my life and to trust your timing and plan. I want to know you the way you want me to know you, and I want to become the person you want me to be.

What have you seen God do in your life during
your times of waiting?

August 4

HE COMES CLOSE

Come close to God, and God will come close to you (James 4:8, NLT).

Lord God, I'm humbled that you would desire a relationship with me and want to be near me. I long for intimacy with you, Lord, but sometimes I erect barriers that keep you away.

Forgive me for allowing unconfessed sin to separate us. When I turn away from the things that displease you, I turn closer to you. Forgive me for being double-minded and for putting other things or myself before you. You don't want to share my attention with anyone or anything else. Forgive me for the times I've been distracted and forgotten how essential your Word and prayer are for getting to know you. Forgive me for not thanking you and praising you more. Forgive me for running to other things to meet my needs.

Thank you for giving me the wonderful opportunity to come close to you, Lord. May I do my part so you can do yours.

How close are you to God right now?

August 5

CREATOR

In the beginning God created the heavens and the earth
(Genesis 1:1, NIV).

God, I'm in awe of you. How do I begin to comprehend your majestic power? You created the heavens and the earth and everything in them, and all you created you sustain. When I ponder the intricate detail and exceptional beauty of all you designed, I can't help but say, "WOW!"

May I never become dulled to your amazing handiwork, Lord. May I never lose my sense of wonderment and excitement of the things you made for me to enjoy. May I always be tuned in to the WOW factor, for you are a WOW God. I praise you for being an awesome God.

When was the last time you said, "WOW!"
to your creative God?

August 6

At My Right Hand

I keep my eyes always on the LORD.
With him at my right hand, I will not be shaken (Psalm 16:8, NIV).

God, at times I forget. If I don't keep something in front of me or at the top of my pile, it's gone from my mind. That's why I have Post-it Notes on my computer and kitchen cabinets and bathroom mirror. Likewise, I need to keep you always before me.

I've learned that whatever I focus on becomes magnified. I want you to be magnified in my life, Lord, not the hardships and trials that have piled up. The troubles can't shake me when I remember that you're at my right hand. Because you're with me, I have strength to meet any circumstances I experience. I have no cause for worry or for fear. May I always turn my head to the right, Lord. Thank you for being there.

Where are your eyes?

August 7

JESUS TOUCHES LEPERS

A man with leprosy came and knelt before him and said,
"Lord, if you are willing, you can make me clean."
Jesus reached out his hand and touched the man. "I am willing,"
He said. "Be clean!" Immediately he was cleansed of his leprosy
(Matthew 8:2-3, NIV).

Jesus, I'm moved by the leper's faith. He knew you had the authority
and power to heal him. He knew you wouldn't cast him aside like
other people did. So this defiled and unclean man—an untouchable–
came and knelt before you with his request.

And you! What an amazing, tender, compassionate God you are!
You could have healed him by just saying, "Be healed." But you
reached out and touched him. You knew how he longed to be
touched. You knew how he longed to be seen and heard and
welcomed. You understood his physical, emotional, and spiritual
needs, and you met every one of them. What a beautiful picture
this is of how you care for all those who come to you in faith.
Thank you, precious Jesus!

How does Jesus' healing of the leper touch you?

August 8

HE'S THE ONE

He covers the heavens with clouds,
provides rain for the earth,
and makes the grass grow in mountain pastures (Psalm 147:8, NLT).

You're the one who made the heavens.

You're the one who covers the heavens with clouds.

You're the one who fills the clouds with rain.

You're the one who created the earth that receives the rain.

You're the one who created the mountains that rise from the earth.

You're the one who makes the grass grow in mountain pastures
because of the rain you send.

You're the one who planned it all, and you're the one who has a plan
for my life.

There's no one like you, God!

What do you think of God's plans?

August 9

ALL CREATION PRAISES

Praise the LORD!
Praise the LORD from the heavens!
Praise him from the skies!
Praise him, all his angels!
Praise him, all the armies of heaven!
Praise him, sun and moon!
Praise him, all you twinkling stars!
Praise him, skies above!
Praise him, vapors high above the clouds!
Let every created thing give praise to the LORD,
for he issued his command, and they came into being
(Psalm 148:1-5, NLT).

I ascribe to you glory and strength, Lord. I ascribe to you the glory due your name. I will worship you in the splendor of your holiness.

You deserve a continual standing ovation, for you—the Lord God omnipotent—reign forever. You are King of kings and Lord of lords, the supreme authority over all the universe. You are majestic in power, brilliant in creation, and dazzling in your splendor.

The angels, armies of heaven, sun and moon, twinkling stars, skies, vapors high above the clouds, and all created things—including me— join together in a symphony of praise to celebrate your greatness. What a privilege it is to honor you as my God.

How does this speak to your soul?

August 10

UNYIELDING STRENGTH AND PEACE

*The Lord will give [unyielding and impenetrable] strength to His
people; the Lord will bless His people with peace (Psalm 29:11, AMP).*

Lord, David wrote these words while weathering a violent
thunderstorm. He knew your presence was his source of strength and
peace to help him endure the fury he faced. He trusted you to give it
to him, and you did.

Thank you that when I come to you, as David did in the midst of the
storm, you give me unyielding and impenetrable strength. You calm
my anxious heart with your blessing of peace.

When my loved one's diagnosis is heartbreaking, you give strength
and peace. When the bills are larger than my budget, you give
strength and peace. When demands pressure me from every side, you
give strength and peace. When people turn against me for no reason,
you give strength and peace. When the enemy gets more and more
creative with his attacks, you give strength and peace. All praise to
you, my God of strength and peace!

*In what situations could you use God's
strength and peace right now?*

August 11
DRY GROUND

When the people broke camp to cross the Jordan, the priests carrying the ark of the covenant went ahead of them. Now the Jordan is at flood stage all during harvest. Yet as soon as the priests who carried the ark reached the Jordan and their feet touched the water's edge, the water from upstream stopped flowing. It piled up in a heap a great distance away, at a town called Adam in the vicinity of Zarethan, while the water flowing down to the Sea of the Arabah (that is, the Dead Sea) was completely cut off. So the people crossed over opposite Jericho. The priests who carried the ark of the covenant of the LORD stopped in the middle of the Jordan and stood on dry ground, while all Israel passed by until the whole nation had completed the crossing on dry ground (Joshua 3:14-17, NIV).

God, you work in supernatural ways when your children walk forward in trust and obedience to you. May I never be afraid of getting my feet wet.

What has been your experience with "touching the water's edge"?

August 12

LIGHT OF THE WORLD

When Jesus spoke again to the people, he said, "I am the light of the world. Whoever follows me will never walk in darkness, but will have the light of life" (John 8:12, NIV).

I praise you for being my light, Jesus. When my life was dark with sin, you brought me into your light and provided what I needed to grow in you.

When the trials I face seem more than I can bear, the rays of your presence comfort me. When I don't know which path to take, or have an important decision to make, you light the way for the next step. When the media reports nothing but chaos and hopelessness, you remind me that you're still shining.

Jesus, your presence gives life and energy. It warms, promotes growth, welcomes, guides, reveals, and brightens days. Thanks for leaving the light on.

How does the Light help you?

August 13
WARRIOR JEHOVAH

The Lord is a warrior—Yes, Jehovah is his name (Exodus 15:3, TLB).

Jehovah, I praise you for being a mighty warrior. You are a master strategist and tactician—superior in strength, power, influence, and creativity. You outthink and outsmart the enemy. No one can match your unique methods for winning battles.

You walled up the Red Sea for your people to cross in safety, and then swallowed their pursuers when you released the waters from your hands. With trumpet sounds and shouting men, you brought down city walls. By men blowing horns and smashing empty jars, you overthrew enemy forces. You took down a giant with a boy, a slingshot, and a stone. As your people sang praises to you, you set ambushes that caused three opposing armies to destroy each other.

You defeated the power of death with an old, rugged cross.

Lord Jehovah, I'm thankful that you are the one who fights my battles. You can handle anything I face.

What do you think of God's approach to fighting battles?

August 14

PEACE OF GOD

Do not be anxious about anything, but in every situation, by prayer and petition, with thanksgiving, present your requests to God. And the peace of God, which transcends all understanding, will guard your hearts and your minds in Christ Jesus (Philippians 4:6-7, NIV).

God, I don't like the way my insides are churning right now. The stress of my situation is too much for me to handle. I just want to have a break down and then sink into oblivion. But this is reality. I can't change what's happening, and I can't hide. Rather than letting anxiety torment me, I come to you. It's not always easy, Lord, but I will pray with thanksgiving because that's my gateway to peace.

Thank you for your care and concern. Thank you for your goodness, faithfulness, and love. Thank you for guarding my heart and mind in Christ Jesus. Thank you that I can trust you with everything. Nothing is too big for you to accomplish or too small for your attention. Thank you for changing my perspective as I focus on you. Thank you for calming my spirit.

In what situations do you find it hard to have peace?

August 15

THRONE OF GRACE

We do not have a high priest who is unable to empathize with our
weaknesses, but we have one who has been tempted in every way,
just as we are—yet he did not sin. Let us then approach God's throne
of grace with confidence, so that we may receive mercy and
find grace to help us in our time of need (Hebrews 4:15-16, NIV).

Lord, you have all power and authority, yet you invite me to approach
your throne with confidence. What a privilege to have that honor!
What a privilege to have your undivided attention!

With assurance of your great love and that you're fully able to meet
my needs, I can come to you with anything that's on my heart,
whether it's a desire, a concern, something I'm struggling with, or an
impossible situation. Because you've experienced life as a human, you
empathize with me and extend your mercy and grace.

Thank you for welcoming me so graciously into your presence, Lord.
And thank you for caring about what I have to say. I love you.

How do you feel knowing you're welcomed to approach
God's throne of grace with confidence?

August 16

RIVERS OF LIVING WATER

On the last and greatest day of the festival, Jesus stood and said in a loud voice, "Let anyone who is thirsty come to me and drink. Whoever believes in me, as Scripture has said, rivers of living water will flow from within them." By this he meant the Spirit, whom those who believed in him were later to receive. Up to that time the Spirit had not been given, since Jesus had not yet been glorified (John 7:37-39, NIV).

Jesus, I have an unquenchable thirst in my soul that only you can satisfy. Thank you for inviting me to come to you to drink and for filling me with your presence through the gift of your Holy Spirit.

Your Spirit wells up in me like a river of living water, generating irrepressible life and energy. As I continue to drink from you, the river overflows and refreshes those in its path. All around me people are dying of thirst, Jesus. I need to point them to you, the source of living water. May my supply be always fresh and never stagnant.

Are your rivers overflowing or dry?

August 17

SHIELD OF FAVOR

Surely, Lord, you bless the righteous;
you surround them with your favor as with a shield (Psalm 5:12, NIV).

Lord, I'm overwhelmed by your goodness to me. I'm blessed because
you see me as righteous. But the only reason I'm considered
righteous is because Jesus' robe of salvation encompasses me.
And I wear his robe of salvation only because I trust in your
great love that sent him to the cross.

You surround me with your favor, Lord. I can't get away from it.
Everything I am and everything I have is the result of your excessive
kindness to me. I don't deserve any of it, but you layer blessing upon
blessing in my life. Your love can't be explained, only experienced.
I'm grateful beyond words.

How has God blessed you?

August 18

STRENGTH OF CHARACTER

We can rejoice, too, when we run into problems and trials, for we know that they are good for us—they help us learn to be patient. And patience develops strength of character in us and helps us trust God more each time we use it until finally our hope and faith are strong and steady. Then, when that happens, we are able to hold our heads high no matter what happens and know that all is well, for we know how dearly God loves us, and we feel this warm love everywhere within us because God has given us the Holy Spirit to fill our hearts with his love (Romans 5:3-5, TLB).

I want to skip the hard stuff, Lord, but I'll rejoice in it because it strengthens my character. If the way were plain and easy, I'd have no need for confidence in you. And when I trust in you I learn about your character and how much you love me. That's how my hope and faith become strong and steady. Thank you for having a purpose in everything, Lord. Even in the problems and trials.

For what problem can you rejoice today?

August 19
FRIEND

I no longer call you slaves, for a master doesn't confide in his slaves; now you are my friends, proved by the fact that I have told you everything the Father told me (John 15:15, TLB).

I'm your friend and you are mine. What a precious thought that is, Jesus! No other friend compares to you. You accept me just the way I am. You believe in me and encourage me to do great things. You're trustworthy and faithful. You never forsake me. You forgive my mistakes—and there are a lot of them! You enjoy being with me, and you make me laugh. No one understands me like you do.

Thank you for sharing your thoughts and for relaying the Father's heart to me. Thank you for being the sunshine in my life. Thank you for always being available for me. I love hanging out with you, Jesus! Thank you for being my best friend.

What do you enjoy most about Jesus' friendship?

August 20

WALKS ON WATER

In the fourth watch [between 3:00—6:00 a.m.] of the night,
Jesus came to them, walking on the sea. And when the disciples saw
Him walking on the sea, they were terrified and said, It is a ghost!
And they screamed out with fright.
But instantly He spoke to them, saying, Take courage! I AM!
Stop being afraid! (Matthew 14:25-27, AMP)

How I love your words to the disciples, Jesus! They're words I need to remember every day. "Take courage! I AM! Stop being afraid!" You're I AM, so I have no reason for fear. I can have courage and confidence in all things because I AM is always present.

Thank you for meeting me in any situation. Not even a stormy sea in the wee hours of the morning can keep you away. There's nothing you can't do. There's nothing you don't care about. I praise you for being I AM in my life.

How does the name I AM encourage you?

August 21

HELP COMES FROM GOD

I lift up my eyes to the mountains—
where does my help come from?
My help comes from the LORD,
the Maker of heaven and earth (Psalm 121:1-2, NIV).

When I need strength or when I need help, I will lift my eyes to you,
the God who
made the heavens, the earth, and the mountains;
holds the stars in place and calls them by name;
ambushes enemy armies;
calms the raging sea;
turns water into wine;
heals the lame and opens the eyes of the blind;
causes demons to tremble; and
raises the dead to life.

There's nothing you can't do. Lord, thank you for inviting me to bring
my burdens and cares to you.

Where does your help come from?

August 22

ALL GLORY TO GOD

All glory to God, who is able to keep you from falling away and will bring you with great joy into his glorious presence without a single fault. All glory to him who alone is God, our Savior through Jesus Christ our Lord. All glory, majesty, power, and authority are his before all time, and in the present, and beyond all time! Amen (Jude 1:24-25, NLT).

All honor goes to you, God, for you are able. You're able to keep me from falling away and will, if I'm willing to let you. Thank you for your Word that guides me. Thank you for drawing near to me when I draw near to you. May I trust you and stay strong in faith.

With joy you're able to bring me into your glorious presence without fault—and that's completely your doing, not mine. Thank you that your great love made it possible through Christ. You're able to receive my praise. May it be a sweet sound in your ear. To you be all glory, majesty, power, and authority today and forevermore.

How will you give glory to your able God today?

August 23
Purposes Unthwarted

"I know that you can do all things;
no purpose of yours can be thwarted" (Job 42:2, NIV).

Lord, you're the God who created me. You're the God who loves me beyond anything I can imagine. You're the God who has things under complete control. No purpose of yours can be thwarted.

You have plans for my life, and I get frustrated when I don't see things happening the way I think they should. I walk forward on what I think is your path and then detours and interruptions impede the process. The tough stuff of life gets in the way. Or does it? Could it be that those things are really working for me?

Your intention for me is to be in right relationship with you and to glorify you. When I trust you in the midst of my trials, I'm fulfilling your purpose. That's how I get to know you, and as I get to know you, you're revealed to others. The way you work is amazing, Lord. Thank you for fulfilling your purpose in me.

What is God doing to fulfill his purpose in your life?

August 24

HE DOESN'T CHANGE

"I am the LORD, and I do not change" (Malachi 3:6a, NLT).

God, I praise you for being constant. In the midst of an always-changing world filled with inconsistent people, I can trust you to be steadfast and sure.

Your love never changes. Your faithfulness never changes. Your goodness never changes. Your grace never changes. Your power never changes. Your ability to heal and perform miracles never changes regardless of what people say. Nothing about you is fickle.

I like knowing what to expect, Lord, and I know what to expect with you. You're the same yesterday, today, and forever. Because of that, I have full assurance that I'm in good hands.

How does knowing God never changes comfort you?

August 25

ROCK AND FORTRESS

I wait quietly before God,
for my victory comes from him.
He alone is my rock and my salvation,
my fortress where I will never be shaken (Psalm 62:1-2, NLT).

Wait quietly? What's that, Lord? There's always something to do, someone who needs me, responsibilities weighing me down, and problems to deal with. My life is hurry, hurry, hurry, spin, spin, spin. Who has time to wait quietly? Sadly, that's how I feel sometimes in the craziness that's my life, and I lose sight of who you are and how you want to help me. Forgive me, Lord.

When I take the time to wait quietly before you, I find strength for what I face daily. I hear your voice, and you gently remind me that you are the one who gives me victory over all the things that have me hurrying and spinning. You alone are my rock and my salvation, my fortress where I won't be shaken. You won't leave me alone or fail me. Help me to stop and wait quietly before you, Lord. You are where I'll find my rest.

How do you do with waiting quietly?

August 26

DAILY BURDEN-BEARER

Praise be to the Lord, to God our Savior,
who daily bears our burdens (Psalm 68:19, NIV).

I praise you, my Lord. I praise you, my God. I praise you, my Savior, for you daily bear my burdens. Every single day. 24/7. You invite me to come to you, and you promise to give me rest when I do. You tell me to cast all my cares and anxieties on you because you care for me.

You want to lighten my load, so it would be silly for me not to take you up on that offer—especially since I can't handle the weight alone. Why would I want to forfeit the peace and needlessly bear the pain? You are a kind, compassionate friend, Lord. What a privilege it is to carry everything to you in prayer.

What burdens can you trust God with today?

August 27
RAINBOW OF PROMISE

Then God said, "I am giving you a sign of my covenant with you and with all living creatures, for all generations to come. I have placed my rainbow in the clouds. It is the sign of my covenant with you and with all the earth. When I send clouds over the earth, the rainbow will appear in the clouds, and I will remember my covenant with you and with all living creatures. Never again will the floodwaters destroy all life. When I see the rainbow in the clouds, I will remember the eternal covenant between God and every living creature on earth"
(Genesis 9:12-16, NLT).

Lord, this promise you made thousands of years ago still holds true today. When I put my trust in you, I'm putting it in a faithful, reliable God. Thank you for being true to your word. Always.

How are you encouraged by the rainbow?

August 28

FOOLISH SHAME

Think of what you were when you were called. Not many of you were
wise by human standards; not many were influential; not many were
of noble birth. But God chose the foolish things of the world to shame
the wise; God chose the weak things of the world to shame the strong
(1 Corinthians 1:26-27, NIV).

God, you make me smile. I love the way you work! Only you could
take a simple, imperfect, underdog of a person like me—with faults,
failures, and weaknesses—and use her to do mighty things for you.

I'm not wise, influential, or of noble birth, but I'm devoted to you. I'm
ready and willing for you to use me, and I'm crazy enough to say yes
to anything you ask. That's all it takes. Once the power of the Holy
Spirit takes over, there's no stopping what can happen.

I delight in being a "foolish and weak thing" in your hands, Lord. May
you receive all honor and glory and praise for the amazing ways you
shame the wise and strong through me.

In what ways have you seen God use foolish things
to shame the wise?

August 29
HE CARES FOR ME

LORD, what are human beings that you care for them,
mere mortals that you think of them? (Psalm 144:3, NIV)

Lord, you deserve the highest honor, and you're worthy of all my praise. I worship you because you are most high, almighty, creator, glorious, magnificent, unequaled God. When I think of who you are, I am but a speck in comparison.

How is it possible that you would care for me? How is it possible that you would love me and cherish me and value me? It makes no sense, Lord. But I'm grateful.

Thank you for your attention. Thank you for your safe keeping. Thank you for your shelter. Thank you for your provision. Thank you for your comforting presence. Thank you for the joy and peace I'm able to have through you in spite of difficulties. Thank you for hope. Thank you that your care package is complete. I love you for who you are and for all you do.

How does knowing that the Almighty God
cares for you impact you?

August 30
THE POTTER

O Lord, you are our Father.
We are the clay, and you are the potter.
We all are formed by your hand (Isaiah 64:8, NLT).

Father, as I look at the assortment of pottery I have, I think about how unique and special the individual pieces are. Each one was designed for a purpose and was fashioned with great care for that purpose by the potter. Although the vases and bowls and pots are different, they have similar distinguishing qualities in workmanship and design that point to the artist who created them.

In the same way, you are forming me into a one-of-a-kind piece of pottery with a particular purpose. The process isn't always easy, because you have to knead me, shape me, reshape me, and put me through the fire, but when you're done I'll be a masterpiece—one that has your fingerprints all over it. Have your way with me, Lord. Mold me and make me according to your good will, and may I be pliable clay in your hands.

How is the work the Potter is doing in your life shaping up?

August 31
GIFT OF GOD

The wages of sin is death, but the free gift of God is eternal life
through Christ Jesus our Lord (Romans 6:23, NLT).

God, how I praise you for your wonderful gifts! How I praise you for Jesus Christ, my Lord! How I praise you for eternal life! How I praise you for a tiny, three-letter word! B-u-t. That changes everything.

I deserve death. Instead, I get life because of Jesus' work on the cross. What a deal! Thank you for giving me the opportunity to trust in Jesus. Thank you for the opportunity for a forever relationship with you. I love you more than I can express, Lord, and I'm grateful that your plan for my life includes the "but."

How has the "but" changed your life?

September

So if you faithfully obey the commands

I am giving you today—to love the L{ORD}

your God and to serve him with all your heart

and with all your soul—then I will send rain

on your land in its season, both autumn

and spring rains, so that you may gather in

your grain, new wine and olive oil.

DEUTERONOMY 11:13-14, NIV

September 1

GREAT IS THE LORD

Great is the LORD and most worthy of praise;
his greatness no one can fathom (Psalm 145:3, NIV).

Lord, I'm in awe of your majesty, and I lift your name on high. You are great and most worthy of praise. How do I even begin to express the magnitude of who you are and what you do? You're King of the ages, King of heaven, and King of glory. Heaven is your throne and earth is your footstool. You alone are the eternal, sovereign God.

You measured the waters in the hollow of your hand and with the breadth of your hand marked off the heavens. You form the mountains, create the wind, turn dawn to darkness, and tread on the heights of the earth.

Your ability is endless. Your greatness knows no bounds. And your love for me transcends all understanding. Blessed be your glorious name. May it be exalted in all the earth.

How will you praise God for his greatness?

September 2

EVERYTHING NEEDED FOR GODLY LIVING

By his divine power, God has given us everything we need for living a
godly life. We have received all of this by coming to know him,
the one who called us to himself by means of his marvelous glory
and excellence (2 Peter 1:3, NLT).

God, I praise you for your marvelous glory and excellence that
called me to you! I praise you for your divine power! Thank you for
the privilege of holy intimacy and for your wonderful gifts. I have
everything I need to live for you and to walk in your ways. I have
everything I need to do the things you ask of me.

I'm grateful for your always-sufficient grace that helps me through
my times of trials. I'm grateful for your strength when I'm weak.
I'm grateful for your empowering to do things beyond my ability.
I'm grateful for your Holy Spirit that guides me in truth and for the
revelation and wisdom I receive. I'm grateful for your Word and your
precious promises. May I honor you by living my life your way.

How has God equipped you to live life his way?

September 3

FRIENDSHIP WITH GOD

Friendship with God is reserved for those who reverence him.
With them alone he shares the secrets of his promises
(Psalm 25:14, TLB).

I love you, Lord. I delight in worshiping you and enjoy your presence in my life. I'm honored that you would call me your friend and share the secrets of your promises. Thank you for allowing me to feel at home with you and for "sharing your couch" with me. I realize that not everyone is given that privilege. It's all because of our special covenant relationship.

The more time I spend with you, the more I recognize your goodness in my life. You reveal your love and favor in ways I hadn't known before. Your Word makes more sense, and I better understand how you work. I'm grateful that you want to show me your ways, teach me your truths, and guide me in your paths. Lord, I want to be so tight with you that it's evident in everything I do. May it be so, Lord. May it be so.

How much time have you spent "on the couch" with God lately?

September 4

FIRST AND LAST

"This is what the LORD says—
Israel's King and Redeemer, the LORD Almighty:
I am the first and I am the last;
apart from me there is no God" (Isaiah 44:6, NIV).

Lord, how I praise you for being my God!

Thank you for being my King.
I'm blessed to have a part in your eternal kingdom.

Thank you for being my Redeemer.
Because of you I'm free and full of life.

Thank you for your almighty hand at work on my behalf.
You sustain me, provide for me, and empower me to
do the important things you've called me to do.

You are the first and the last, and you control everything in between.
No one can take your place.

I worship you. I delight in you. I'm honored to receive your love.

How does this verse speak to you today?

September 5

ALWAYS ON GUARD

The LORD will keep you from all harm—
he will watch over your life;
the LORD will watch over your coming and going
both now and forevermore (Psalm 121:7-8, NIV).

God, I praise you for being my all-seeing God. Your eyes are always on me. As I come or as I go, you're on the lookout, guarding me and protecting me. Your eyes are sharper than those of a mother watching her young child on a playground full of bigger kids. You're more alert than the men in black surrounding the President.

During the day, you go before me, clearing a path to keep me safe. Late at night when no one else can see a threat, you're wide awake. Your Spirit hovers over me like a shield. You guard my heart; you guard my body. Nothing can touch my life without your permission. Because I'm secure on your watch, I can rest.

How are you comforted in knowing that God watches your coming and going?

September 6

THE GREAT EXCHANGE

God took the sinless Christ and poured into him our sins. Then,
in exchange, he poured God's goodness into us!
(2 Corinthians 5:21, TLB)

God, I can't thank you enough for your great exchange.
How is it possible that the sinless Christ would bear the punishment
and pain for sinful, undeserving me? You put my wrong on him so I
could be right with you. I'll never understand your love for me, and
I'll never be able to repay you for your goodness. May I show my
gratitude by honoring you with my trust and obedience,
and may I glorify your name in all I do.

What's your response to God's great exchange?

September 7

He Opens Minds

He opened their minds so they could understand the Scriptures
(Luke 24:45, NIV).

Lord, how I thank you for the gift of your Word! How wonderful that you—the Author—would open my mind so I could understand the messages you have for me there.

Thank you for the guidance of your Holy Spirit as I read. Thank you for revealing yourself to me so I can know you better. Thank you for showing me your hidden treasures. Thank you for pointing out truths to counteract the lies of the world. Thank you for reminding me of your promises. Thank you for making your Word alive and new for each day. Thank you for bubbling up the exact communication I need from you at the proper times. May my mind be open to your insights, my ears open to your voice, and my heart receptive to knowledge of you.

What has God recently opened your mind to see in his Word?

September 8

HIS POWER IS GREAT

The LORD is slow to get angry, but his power is great,
and he never lets the guilty go unpunished.
He displays his power in the whirlwind and the storm.
The billowing clouds are the dust beneath his feet.
The LORD is good,
a strong refuge when trouble comes.
He is close to those who trust in him (Nahum 1:3,7, NLT).

Lord, I tremble at the thought of your great power and what you're able to do. You display your mighty force in the whirlwind and the storm. The earth quakes at your voice, the oceans rage, and the mountains shake. I wouldn't want to be the object of your wrath.

You never let the guilty go unpunished, yet for those who trust in you, you are a refuge when trouble comes. You show your goodness and treat them with gentleness and kindness. Thank you for being my safe place, Lord. Thank you for being close. Thank you for looking on me in love. And thank you for your gift of grace that made it possible.

What are your thoughts about how God shows
his power and goodness?

September 9

TRULY FREE

"I tell you the truth, everyone who sins is a slave of sin. A slave is not a permanent member of the family, but a son is part of the family forever. So if the Son sets you free, you are truly free"
(John 8:34-36, NLT).

Jesus, you came to earth to proclaim liberty for the prisoners and to set the oppressed free. Thank you for holding the key to my freedom and for replacing my shackles with wings.

Now that I'm truly free and no longer bound by sin, I want to walk in truth. Help me to adhere to your teachings and to live in accordance with your will. May I stay focused on you and throw off anything that tries to hinder our relationship.

How does freedom feel to you?

September 10

REFUGE AND STRONGHOLD

The LORD is a refuge for the oppressed,
a stronghold in times of trouble.
Those who know your name trust in you,
for you, LORD, have never forsaken those who seek you
(Psalm 9:9-10, NIV).

Lord, how thankful I am for your welcoming arms! When I'm in the midst of trouble and my life is in upheaval, I can run to you and know I'm safe and secure. My circumstances right now are overwhelming, Lord, and I can't face them alone. The only thing I can do is cling to you and trust you to work things out.

You are all-knowing and all-seeing, and you have infinite wisdom. When I'm in your comforting presence, I can rest in the knowledge of who you are and what you're able to do. Your plans for me are good. I praise you for being my refuge, my stronghold, and my savior. You are faithful in your care and mighty in power. Thank you for never turning me away.

How has God been your place of refuge and stronghold
in times of trouble?

September 11

SHELTER OF THE MOST HIGH

Whoever dwells in the shelter of the Most High
will rest in the shadow of the Almighty (Psalm 91:1, NIV).

Most high, almighty God, in you I live and move and have my being.
I love you, and I rejoice in the rest that comes from dwelling in you.
Thank you for your shelter, Lord. I don't know what I'd do without
your strong presence in my life. You are my refuge and fortress,
my God in whom I trust. I don't need to fear terror, pestilence, or
destruction because I'm safe in the protection of your mighty wing.
Your faithfulness acts as my shield, and your presence gives me the
strength and stability I need to carry on.

Thank you for answering when I cry out to you. Thank you for being
with me in times of trouble. Thank you for promising to rescue me. I
praise you for being my salvation and place of sweet peace.

What helps you to dwell in the shelter of the Most High?

September 12

HE FOILS AND THWARTS

The LORD foils the plans of the nations;
he thwarts the purposes of the peoples (Psalm 33:10, NIV).

I praise you, Lord, for you are the almighty, the everlasting, and sovereign God. You are the King of nations and ruler of heaven and earth. Despite the wicked actions and chaos stirred up in the world by selfish people, corrupt governments, and antagonistic nations, you will always be in control. Your plans are for good and not evil, and your purposes will prevail.

No matter what the media reports or how things appear, I choose to remember that you work in supernatural and imaginative ways. You created all things, and you can use anything you created to work on your behalf. Just as you manipulated the weather and set ambushes to foil the plans and thwart the purposes of those who went against your will in the past, you can do so today.

I don't understand your ways, Lord, but I can trust you because I know you. You are my able, unshakable God. I'm thankful that my life is in your hands.

What is your takeaway from today's words?

September 13

JESUS FORGIVES

Two other men, both criminals, were also led out with him to be executed. When they came to the place called the Skull, they crucified him there, along with the criminals—one on his right, the other on his left. Jesus said, "Father, forgive them, for they do not know what they are doing." And they divided up his clothes by casting lots (Luke 23:32-34, NIV).

Jesus, I'm in awe of your compassion and concern for those who don't know you. You were condemned to die for committing no sin, yet you were willing to forgive those who did it to you. It didn't matter what they'd done. You looked beyond their actions and saw their innermost needs. Of most importance to you was their eternal souls, and you showed empathy by understanding their ignorance of their own great crime.

Thank you for similarly showing your compassion and concern for me and for welcoming me into an eternal relationship with you. May I remember your example and extend the same mercy to the ignorant people in my life.

How can you show compassion and concern for the ignorant people in your life?

September 14

THE LORD SEARCHES

*"The eyes of the LORD search the whole earth in order to strengthen
those whose hearts are fully committed to him"
(2 Chronicles 16:9, NLT).*

Lord, I praise you for your divine radar and x-ray vision. You're always
on the lookout for those whose hearts are committed to you, and you
show yourself strong on their behalf.

I'm grateful that you're not impressed with fancy résumés, top-notch
credentials, and outward appearances as the world is. It's what's below
the surface that gets your attention. You care about thoughts, attitudes,
desires, and motives, and when you find someone whose heart is set on
you, you demonstrate your strength, grace, and power in their life.

Thank you that my longing to know you better and my desire
to please you don't go unnoticed. Thank you for not expecting
perfection on my part and for giving me what I need to grow in my
relationship with you. I look forward to receiving all that you have
prepared for me. I love you, Lord.

What kind of heart does God see in you?

September 15

WHO IS LIKE HIM?

"Who is like you among the gods, O LORD—
glorious in holiness,
awesome in splendor,
performing great wonders?" (Exodus 15:11, NLT)

O Lord, I praise you for being unlike all other gods. I praise you for being my God! You are glorious in holiness and deserving of honor. No god or created being can compare. You are awesome in splendor. The heavens and earth display your magnificence and grandeur.

You perform great wonders and are capable of doing things far beyond the confines of my imagination. Your right hand has limitless power. The sun, moon, and stars proclaim your majesty. The winds and the waves obey your commands, and the demons tremble at your name.

I extol you, Lord, for you are the highly exalted, almighty, living God. How I rejoice in the privilege of relationship with you!

In what ways is God unlike any other god?

September 16

ALIVE WITH CHRIST

*Because of his great love for us, God, who is rich in mercy, made us
alive with Christ even when we were dead in transgressions—it is by
grace you have been saved (Ephesians 2:4-5, NIV).*

God, how is it you love me so much that you don't hold my sins
against me? I'm the one who has wronged you and should be dead
in my transgressions, yet you came up with a plan for me to
live—and to live fully!

It's incomprehensible to me that you would have your only Son take
the death blow on my behalf. But you are a God who is rich in mercy,
and because of your grace I'm freed from the holds that sin had on me.

Thank you for your beautiful gift of forgiveness, Lord. I don't need
to work for it or repay it. I get to just receive it and rejoice in what it
means for me. Life. Abundant life. A forever life in relationship with
you. May I bring you pleasure by living each day in gratitude.

What does it mean to you to be alive in Christ?

September 17

INCOMPARABLE

With whom, then, will you compare God?
To what image will you liken him? (Isaiah 40:18, NIV)

No one is like you, Lord. You are great, and your name is mighty in power. You're not made in the form of anything in heaven above, the earth beneath, or waters below. Instead, you're the one who spoke all things into existence.

You're not cast in silver or gold, nor are you chiseled from a chunk of wood. You're not an idol with a mouth that can't speak or eyes that can't see. You're not an inanimate god that can't hear, smell, feel, or walk. No! You, oh Lord, are full of life and your Spirit inhabits those who love you.

You won't topple, melt in a furnace, or burn in a fire. You don't sit in a corner or on a shelf or in a shrine. You are indescribable, uncontainable, unshakable, incomparable, and worthy of all honor and praise. As for me, rather than serve a worthless fraud that can't save, I choose to trust in you—the true, living, eternal God. I worship you, Lord.

How are you blessed in relationship with the true God?

September 18

STRONG FORTRESS

The name of the LORD is a strong fortress;
the godly run to him and are safe (Proverbs 18:10, NLT).

Jehovah—I AM THAT I AM—your name is a strong fortress. An all-powerful defense in times of peril. When I run to you, you elevate me high above the surrounding danger and keep me safe within your walls of love. You are a tower of refuge for those who put their trust in you. The ultimate deliverer. Anyone who calls on you will be saved.

There's only one place I know of that is unconquerable, unassailable, and beyond the reach of this world's curse. It's as close as the whisper of your name—the name above all others. You, oh Lord, are great and greatly to be praised! Thank you for being my place of escape.

How is the name of the Lord a strong fortress for you?

September 19

My God will liberally supply (fill to the full) your every need according to His riches in glory in Christ Jesus (Philippians 4:19, AMP).

Lord, I praise you for not being a half-way God. You liberally supply my every need according to your abundant riches. Because I trust in you, I've never lacked food, shelter, or clothing, and I always have countless things for which to be thankful. I'm grateful for the many sweet surprises you send my way during the lean times, and I love your creativity in providing. You are a good God who works beyond the realm of my limited thinking.

As the news reports grow dimmer each day, and the media are generous with their dire economic predictions, I rejoice that you're not constrained by what's happening in the world. Your well never runs dry. Even with announcements of trouble, I have access to never-ending riches through you, Lord. I praise you that absence of resources is never a problem for a kingdom-minded person. With you there is always more, and there is always hope.

For what provisions will you thank God today?

September 20

His Wisdom, Understanding, and Knowledge

By wisdom the Lord laid the earth's foundations,
by understanding he set the heavens in place;
by his knowledge the watery depths were divided,
and the clouds let drop the dew (Proverbs 3:19-20, NIV).

Lord, there's no escaping your greatness. With wisdom, understanding, and knowledge you laid the foundations of the earth, set the heavens in place, and divided the watery depths. You filled the clouds with dew to nourish what you made. All things came into being and are sustained through you. It's easy to say you originated everything, but my finite mind can't grasp the magnitude of what that means because the vast majority of your work is yet unexplored and left unseen.

As I ponder your creativity and power, and face the truth of who you are, I realize how insignificant my wisdom, understanding, and knowledge are compared to yours. Forgive me for the times I've questioned your plans. Forgive me for my wavering trust. I'm grateful that you desire to teach me your ways, Lord. May I seek to know you more and walk in alignment with your will.

What are your thoughts about God's wisdom,
understanding, and knowledge?

September 21

LIFE AND LIGHT

In him was life, and that life was the light of all mankind
(John 1:4, NIV).

Jesus, I praise you for being the author of life—physical life, spiritual life, abundant life, eternal life. All life comes by the power of your Word. You are the reason for my existence, and you are the reason I will live in a forever relationship with you and your Father.

Thank you for providing all I need to sustain my life, and thank you for your light, which is vital for my growth. I rejoice in life, I rejoice in light, and I rejoice in your love.

How are you impacted by Jesus, the giver of life and light?

September 22

REPAYMENT FOR LOCUST YEARS

"I will repay you for the years the locusts have eaten—
the great locust and the young locust,
the other locusts and the locust swarm" (Joel 2:25, NIV).

Oh God, these words resonate with my soul, and I thank you for the hope they give. I've not experienced the destruction of actual locusts, but I've had seasons of life that have been difficult, and I know the pain of loss and devastation. Right now I don't understand the purpose of the locusts in my life, and I can't figure out your plan, but I trust you to be who you say you are, and to do what you say you will do.

During this time as you work out your purpose and plan, may I open my heart to love you more, may I open my eyes to see you more, and may I open my mind to realize the wonderful truth of who you are: a God who excels in restoration and redemption; a God who abundantly blesses; and a God whose grace abounds.

What hope do you receive in knowing God can repay the
years in your life the locusts have eaten?

September 23

DELIGHT IN HIM

Delight yourself also in the Lord, and He will give you the desires and
secret petitions of your heart (Psalm 37:4, AMP).

Oh Lord, I love loving you, and I celebrate the relationship we have!
You fill my life with joy, hope, dreams, and promise. Because of you, I
have a song in my heart and a sparkle in my eyes. Only you can satisfy
my deepest longings, Lord. Wealth doesn't, status doesn't, possessions
don't, nor do any of the other temporary things of the world.

As I delight in you, you place in me the desire to know you more, to
love you more, and to experience you more. That's my biggest want,
Lord. I want you. You fulfill me. Everything else you give is a bonus.
Thank you for the way you take pleasure in me. Thank you for shining
your favor on me and for sending heavenly showers of sweet surprises.
You make me smile.

What are the desires and secret petitions of your heart?

September 24

HIS AUTHORITATIVE WORD

The LORD merely spoke,
and the heavens were created.
He breathed the word,
and all the stars were born.
He assigned the sea its boundaries
and locked the oceans in vast reservoirs.
Let the whole world fear the LORD,
and let everyone stand in awe of him.
For when he spoke, the world began!
It appeared at his command (Psalm 33:6-9, NLT).

God, I'm in awe of you and I praise you for your power. Nothing is too hard for you. You simply spoke and the invisible became visible. The magnificent heavens, the brilliant stars, the seas, the oceans, the world—all instantly appeared and positioned themselves at your command.

As I think about the authority your Word carries, Lord, I wonder what you could do with me and through me if I obeyed you immediately. What visible things could you bring forth from the invisible things in my life? What would manifest at your command if I would readily work in alignment with your will? I look forward to what you want to create in me. May I please you by eagerly responding to your voice.

What does God want to create in you?

September 25

PROMISES FULFILLED

The LORD gave to Israel all the land he had sworn to give their ancestors, and they took possession of it and settled there. And the LORD gave them rest on every side, just as he had solemnly promised their ancestors. Not a single one of all the good promises the LORD had given to the family of Israel was left unfulfilled; everything he had spoken came true (Joshua 21:43-45, NLT).

I praise you, Lord, for you keep your promises. Every word you speak comes true. You are a faithful and trustworthy God. Thank you for the promises you've given me. I look forward to all you have in store.

May I please you by not wavering in unbelief but by stepping into the promises and moving forward in trust, regardless of how circumstances appear. May I keep my eyes and heart set on you, and when I'm tempted to get discouraged that things don't unfold in my timeframe, help me to remember that you don't forget.

What are some of the promises you're waiting for the Lord to fulfill?

September 26

THE HOLY SPIRIT

The Comforter (Counselor, Helper, Intercessor, Advocate, Strengthener, Standby), the Holy Spirit, Whom the Father will send in My name [in My place, to represent Me and act on My behalf], He will teach you all things. And He will cause you to recall (will remind you of, bring to your remembrance) everything I have told you (John 14:26, AMP).

Holy Spirit, what a gift you are to me! Thank you for connecting with my spirit and for the many ways you act on my behalf. Knowing that you live with me and dwell in me brings great comfort.

I'm blessed by the way you usher me into the presence of the Father and for the important truths you teach me about him. Not only do you teach me, but you remind me as well! I'm grateful that when I can't trust myself to recall details, I can trust you to whisper them to me at the needed times.

I praise you for being my advisor, exhorter, comforter, strengthener, intercessor, encourager, teacher, helper, and guide. But most of all, I thank you for being my friend.

What do you most appreciate about the Holy Spirit's work in your life?

September 27

HIS COMPASSION AND MERCY

The LORD is compassionate and merciful,
slow to get angry and filled with unfailing love.
He will not constantly accuse us,
nor remain angry forever.
He does not punish us for all our sins;
he does not deal harshly with us, as we deserve (Psalm 103:8-10, NLT).

Lord, how I thank you for not punishing me for all my sins!
How I thank you for not dealing harshly with me, as I deserve!
How I thank you that you don't remain angry forever!
How I thank you that you won't constantly accuse me!
What great relief and peace I have in knowing that.

I praise you for being a compassionate and merciful God. Even with
all my shortcomings and offenses, you are slow to get angry. Your
mercies are new every morning. Your love never fails, and you never
give up on me. I'm grateful for your kindness and goodness to me,
Lord. May I honor you with my devotion and obedience.

How does God's compassion and mercy bless you?

September 28

TRANSGRESSIONS BLOTTED OUT

I, even I, am He Who blots out and cancels your transgressions, for My own sake, and I will not remember your sins (Isaiah 43:25, AMP).

Lord, I'm a humbled and grateful recipient of your mercy. You choose to erase your memory of my sins. I have no words to say but *thank you!*

Thank you! Thank you! Thank you!

What's your response to God's mercy?

September 29

FULL OF GOD

For in Christ there is all of God in a human body; so you have everything when you have Christ, and you are filled with God through your union with Christ. He is the highest Ruler, with authority over every other power (Colossians 2:9-10, TLB).

Jesus, I praise you for being the highest ruler. You have authority over every other power. In you is all of God, and I have everything because I have you. You complete me.

Thank you for the blessing of relationship with you, and thank you that through our union, I'm filled with God. I'm grateful that the closer I grow to you, the more you radiate from my life.

I want to impact others, Lord. I want people to see you in my actions, in my eyes, and in my smile. I want them to be attracted to God within me and to be curious about why I'm different than most. May I please you by my desires, Jesus. Help me to change the atmosphere wherever I go because of your presence within me.

What does it mean to you to be full of God?

September 30

HIND'S FEET, HIGH PLACES

He makes my feet like hinds' feet [able to stand firmly or make progress on the dangerous heights of testing and trouble]; He sets me securely upon my high places (Psalm 18:33, AMP).

Thank you for your divine equipping, Lord. You never promised an easy path, but you assured me of your presence and that you could use all things for good in my life. As I look back at the things I've faced over the years, I see how you've developed in me a strength of character I wouldn't have had without trusting you through the tests and troubles. Each crisis I've endured has prepared me for the next and has helped me stand more firmly in my relationship with you.

Thank you for teaching me how to be surefooted in the midst of trials. You keep me balanced in your love, and your steady hand holds me securely as I climb higher and higher on the rocky, slippery trails. I'm grateful for my hinds' feet, Lord, and I praise you for meeting me in high places.

How have the rocky, slippery trials in your life made you more surefooted in your relationship with God?

October

He makes springs pour water into the ravines;

it flows between the mountains.

He waters the mountains from his upper chambers;

the land is satisfied by the fruit of his work.

PSALM 104:10, 13, NIV

October 1

BY HIS GRACE

God saved you by his grace when you believed. And you can't take
credit for this; it is a gift from God. Salvation is not a reward for
the good things we have done, so none of us can boast about it
(Ephesians 2:8-9, NLT).

Lord, I praise you for your marvelous gift of grace that's greater than
all my sin. The life I have right now is only by that grace, which came
to me through faith in you. Today I enjoy the infinite, matchless
blessings of forgiveness, freedom, spiritual riches, abundant life, and
your presence at work in me. I'm humbled by your goodness.

Because grace is your gift to me, there's no striving on my part. No
legalistic rules I have to follow. No long to-do list. All credit for my
salvation goes to you, Lord, and I thank you for the incredible love
that made it possible. I want to live each day in gratitude to you.
May the praise song in my heart bring you joy.

How would your life be different without God's grace?

October 2

A TESTED HELP

God is our refuge and strength, a tested help in times of trouble. And
so we need not fear even if the world blows up and the mountains
crumble into the sea. Let the oceans roar and foam; let the mountains
tremble! (Psalm 46:1-3, TLB)

Lord, I praise you for being my refuge and strength. With the current
state of affairs—a world in upheaval, unsteady weather patterns, viral
breakouts of disease, and unstable personal life circumstances—I'm
grateful for my relationship with you. Because I trust in you, there's no
need for me to fear anything.

When troubles come, whatever they may be, I can run to you and
know I'm protected. No one loves or cares for me the way you do,
Lord, and nothing offers the security that comes from resting in
your warm embrace.

Thank you for hearing my cries. Thank you for listening to my prayers,
and thank you for inviting me to dwell in your shelter—a place of
peace and safety. There will always be trouble, but you will always be
God. I praise you for your ever-present help.

For what troubles do you need God's refuge
and strength today?

October 3

NOT ORPHANED

I will not leave you as orphans [comfortless, desolate, bereaved, forlorn, helpless]; I will come [back] to you (John 14:18, AMP).

Jesus, thank you for your precious promise that you won't leave me as an orphan, and thank you for keeping your word that you won't abandon me. I praise you for your faithfulness.

Parents, family members, and other loved ones have departed from me, and circumstances in my life often lead to a sense of hopelessness and helplessness, but I can count on your presence to be with me at all times. Although I don't see you physically, my heart knows you're here. Daily I receive your comfort, care, and assurance. Your love gives me encouragement and strength to carry on.

I'm grateful, Lord, that your Spirit dwells within me, the Father has adopted me as his own, and I'm a joint heir with you in all he has to give. What joy I receive in being a part of the family of God! I'm eternally blessed.

When have you experienced the feeling of abandonment, and how does Jesus' promise give you hope?

October 4

Victory Over Sin and Death

*Thank God! He gives us victory over sin and death
through our Lord Jesus Christ (1 Corinthians 15:57, NLT).*

How can I help but thank you, God? Jesus met death head-on and
defeated it. That's good news for me! Thank you that Jesus' victory
is my victory. Because I'm in Christ, I get to share in the new life his
victory won. Death may one day take my body, but my spirit will live
forever in relationship with you.

Thank you that sin has lost its power over me. Thank you that when I
set my heart and thoughts on you, you enable me to overcome
in every area of life through Jesus' name. Thank you for giving me
the opportunity to rehearse an old cheer from high school days:
"V-I-C-T-O-R-Y! Victory, victory, that's my cry!" Thank you for allowing
me to celebrate that victory every day by living my life for you.
Victory. Sweet victory.

What does victory over sin and death mean to you?

October 5

THE CERTAINTY OF HIS LOVE

For though the mountains should depart and the hills be shaken or removed, yet My love and kindness shall not depart from you, nor shall My covenant of peace and completeness be removed, says the Lord, Who has compassion on you (Isaiah 54:10, AMP).

Lord, I praise you for who you are—a steadfast God whose promises are certain. It's more likely that the mountains would move and the hills disappear than for your love and kindness to depart from me. Nothing can separate me from your love and kindness, and nothing can diminish it. Other things may be taken away from me, but your love always remains.

I praise you for being a covenant keeper. Your wonderful gifts of peace and completeness will not be removed. I'm grateful for your peace that passes all understanding, and I'm grateful for your calming, reassuring presence when everything around me is in turmoil.

Thank you for your compassion and mercy, Lord. Thank you for your favor. Thank you for your goodness and for the blessing of your smile on my life. I delight in you.

How are you comforted by the certainty of God's love?

October 6

FREEDOM FROM FEAR

I prayed to the LORD, and he answered me.
He freed me from all my fears (Psalm 34:4, NLT).

Lord, I praise you for who you are—a big God who answers prayer and instills courage in his loved ones. When I focus on you rather than the circumstances causing my fear, I realize I have no reason to be afraid. Today I choose to remember that you're always with me, and your name is I AM. I can trust you in all situations because you speak truth and keep your promises.

You're the God who was with David, Moses, and Abraham in times of old, and you're the One who has a purpose and plan for me today. Nothing surprises you. You know all; you see all. You're sovereign, creator, King, and controller. Your power surpasses that of anyone or anything. Demons tremble at the mention of your name. Mountains quake and oceans roar when you speak.

You love me more than anything I can imagine. And you're on my side. Why should I fear? Lord, help me to keep my mind filled with thoughts of you.

What should you remember about God when you're afraid?

October 7

GOD IS INDEED GOD

*"Understand, therefore, that the LORD your God is indeed God. He is
the faithful God who keeps his covenant for a thousand generations
and lavishes his unfailing love on those who love him and obey his
commands" (Deuteronomy 7:9, NLT).*

Lord, I praise you because you are God in heaven above and on earth
below. There is no other. You are indeed God—my God. Thank you
for your faithfulness in keeping your covenants. You promise that if
I love and obey you that you'll lavish your unfailing love on me.
I love being loved by you!

I delight in the way you bless me and keep me and make your face
shine upon me. The favor of your presence gives me peace, joy, hope,
and courage. I worship you for the honor of being your child, Lord.
May I honor you by loving you all the days of my life.

What does the phrase "God is indeed God" mean to you?

October 8

HIS INVISIBLE QUALITIES

*Ever since the world was created, people have seen the earth and
sky. Through everything God made, they can clearly see his invisible
qualities—his eternal power and divine nature. So they have
no excuse for not knowing God (Romans 1:20, NLT).*

The heavens declare your glory, Lord. The skies proclaim the work of
your hands. Day after day they speak of your greatness, and night
after night they display your knowledge. There's no place on earth
where they aren't seen. Evidence of your eternal power and divine
nature is all around me. The radiating sun, the shimmering moon,
and the glowing stars all serve as reminders of your constant
presence and wonderful love.

Signs of your love and goodness come in countless ways, Lord. Help
me to slow down, pay attention, acknowledge you, and acclaim your
excellence. May I use every opportunity I have to direct others to your
invisible qualities so they might know you.

What do you learn about God from all he has made?

October 9

LIKE A FATHER

The Lord is like a father to his children,
tender and compassionate to those who fear him.
For he knows how weak we are;
he remembers we are only dust (Psalm 103:13-14, NLT).

Loving God, my heart is warmed at the thought of you being my Father. My spirit sees the twinkle in your eyes and the smile that lights up your face when you look upon me, and I feel caressed by your tenderness and compassion. I love the way you love me!

You're fully aware of my weaknesses and know how often I mess up, yet you're kind and patient with me. You don't expect perfection or turn your back on me. Instead, you give me the help and guidance I need to learn and grow in you.

You want what's best for me. I'm blessed knowing that you have good plans for my life and a glorious future in store. Thank you for caring about me so deeply, for standing with me through my highs and lows, and for your generous provision. I'm grateful to be your child.

How is God like a father to you?

October 10

WITH ME EVERY STEP

*"Yes, be bold and strong! Banish fear and doubt! For remember, the
Lord your God is with you wherever you go" (Joshua 1:9, TLB).*

Oh God, as I let these words sink in, I'm grateful for the reminder
that you are with me every step I take. I know you have exciting new
things in store for me, and you have me poised for what's next in my
life, but you haven't revealed the whole picture.

It's an uncomfortable spot to be in, and the power of the unknown
messes with my mind. But the way you work isn't unknown to me.
You've proven yourself to me again and again. You've shown me that
you're trustworthy and that there's no better place to be than in the
center of your will.

Help me to trust you more, Lord. I want to be always mindful that
you're present and powerful on my journey. I praise you for being a
mighty, faithful God—the God of my unknowns. Thank you for walking
hand-in-hand with me and for fortifying me with strength and courage.

*When have you needed the reminder that God
is with you every step you take?*

October 11

GOOD SHEPHERD

"I am the good shepherd; the good shepherd lays down His life for the sheep. He who is a hired hand, and not a shepherd, who is not the owner of the sheep, sees the wolf coming, and leaves the sheep and flees, and the wolf snatches them and scatters them. He flees because he is a hired hand and is not concerned about the sheep"
(John 10:11-13, NASB).

Jesus, I praise you for being my good shepherd. As one of your precious lambs, I'm grateful for your tender, compassionate care and safekeeping. I know how much I matter to you, because it's evident by the way you serve me. I'm humbled that you would lay down your life on my behalf. It's hard for me to grasp that kind of love. Thank you for treasuring me the way you do.

Thank you, too, for comforting me with the assurance of your constant presence. You don't run when trouble comes. Instead, you meet trouble head-on and prevent anything from coming near me without your permission. Jesus, my shepherd, I worship and adore you. I'm blessed to be one of your flock.

*How are you blessed as a lamb under the care
of the good shepherd?*

October 12

THE LORD'S DISCIPLINE

My child, don't reject the LORD's discipline,
and don't be upset when he corrects you.
For the LORD corrects those he loves,
just as a father corrects a child in whom he delights
(Proverbs 3:11-12, NLT).

Thank you for loving me so much that you correct me, Lord. I'm not fond of discipline, but I know it's for my good. You do it because you want what's best for me and you have big plans for my future.

Help me to remember that just as parents correct their misguided and disobedient children, you correct me. If you didn't, I'd have to question whether I was really your child. Rather than fighting the discipline, help me to submit to it and learn the valuable lessons you have for me. I want to grow stronger in my faith and closer in my relationship with you.

I'm grateful that you don't give up on me, Lord, and I'm thankful for your wonderful gift of forgiveness. Continue to work in my life so I can be the best me I can be for your honor and glory.

How do you respond to the Lord's discipline?

October 13

HELP FOR TEMPTATION

The only temptation that has come to you is that which everyone has.
But you can trust God, who will not permit you to be tempted more
than you can stand. But when you are tempted, he will also give you
a way to escape so that you will be able to stand it
(1 Corinthians 10:13, NCV).

Lord, I'm grateful that nothing gets past you. You know the trials and temptations I face, and you care. Thank you for the reminder that I'm not the only one who's ever had problems. Many others have, too, and you helped them to endure. You'll do the same for me.

I praise you for being faithful and for being the God of absolutes. You will never let me down. You will never let me be pushed past my limit. You will always be there to help me come through it. Those are great promises, Lord! When I trust you, you give me all I need to bear the testing. Thank you!

What encouragement do you receive
from this promise today?

October 14

GOD REVEALS MYSTERIES

"No wise man, enchanter, magician or diviner can explain to the king the mystery he has asked about, but there is a God in heaven who reveals mysteries" (Daniel 2:27-28a, NIV).

No one is like you, Lord, for you are the God in heaven. You are great, and your name is mighty in power. Among all the wise men, enchanters, magicians, and diviners of the nations, and in all their kingdoms, there is no one who can reveal mysteries but you.

Lord, would you reveal your mysteries to me? I want to know you in deeper ways. Open my eyes to what you are doing and what you have done in and around me. Help me to see beyond the natural realm and experience more of you in the spiritual realm. Reveal yourself and your plans to me as I focus on you.

I'm grateful that when I call to you, you tell me marvelous and wondrous things I'd never have known on my own. May my heavenly receptors be fully-awake to all you have for me.

When are you most receptive to the things God wants to reveal to you?

October 15

He Will Lead and Guide

In your unfailing love you will lead
the people you have redeemed.
In your strength you will guide them
to your holy dwelling (Exodus 15:13, NIV).

Because you love me, Lord, you lead me. You don't expect me to wander aimlessly, trying to find my own way. Instead, you give me everything I need to get to the place you want me to be—your holy dwelling. It's a place of promise, abundance, and rest, and it's a place you have reserved for me.

Thank you for guiding me in your strength. I don't have to strive. As I follow you, without straying off your paths, you show me that your holy dwelling is actually realized in sweet relationship with you.

I praise you for your unfailing love, for leading me, for redeeming me, for strengthening me, for guiding me, and for blessing me with your known presence. You are mine and I am yours. All yours.

What does God's holy dwelling represent to you?

October 16

GOD'S TIMING

Don't forget this, dear friends, that a day or a thousand years from now is like tomorrow to the Lord. He isn't really being slow about his promised return, even though it sometimes seems that way. But he is waiting, for the good reason that he is not willing that any should perish, and he is giving more time for sinners to repent
(2 Peter 3:8-9, TLB).

God, I praise you for being timeless. You're not constrained by seconds, minutes, hours, days, or years as I am. You're an eternal God who works on an eternal schedule. That's hard for me to grasp, especially when I want plans to work according to my schedule—one that includes yesterday, today, or tomorrow, and not a thousand years from now.

Help me to appreciate periods of waiting and to trust you for what you want to accomplish. You're not slow. You are patient. And you have a purpose and plan for everyone, including those who are lost. Thank you for your great compassion, Lord, and for your perfect timing in all things.

What do you think about God's timing?

October 17

COME AND SEE

Come and see what our God has done,
what awesome miracles he performs for people! (Psalm 66:5, NLT)

How awesome are your deeds, God! How great is your power! I shout with joy to you and sing the glory of your name. The Bible is full of extraordinary events that testify to your greatness, and you haven't changed. You continue to be a superior God who works in supernatural ways. I marvel at the unexplainable things you do in my life and in the lives of those around me.

I join with the psalmist David in proclaiming, "I will extol the LORD at all times; his praise will always be on my lips. I will glory in the LORD; let the afflicted hear and rejoice. Glorify the LORD with me; let us exalt his name together" (Psalm 34:1-2, NIV).

I get excited when I see you work, Lord, and I want to invite everyone to come and see what you have done—the awesome miracles you perform for your people. Thank you that the more I tell others, the more you give me to tell. I love bragging on you.

What awesome miracles have you experienced God perform?

October 18

FEAR OF THE LORD

The fear of the Lord is the beginning of wisdom,
and knowledge of the Holy One is understanding (Proverbs 9:10, NIV).

Lord, thank you for teaching me that wisdom doesn't come through
a mechanical formula. It's a result of revering you and putting you
in the proper place in my life. You are the holy, almighty God who
deserves my worship. The wisest thing I can do is to honor you.

I'm delighted that you would give me the privilege of relationship and the
opportunity to know you in intimate ways. As I seek to know you more,
the better I understand what pleases and displeases you. Thank you for
revealing those things to me through your Holy Spirit and your Word.

The wisdom you give benefits me, Lord. It guides, directs, teaches,
protects, and helps me live in accordance with your will. It draws me
closer to you. Fools despise wisdom and instruction. They say in their
hearts that there is no God. I'm grateful I know better. You're my God,
the fount of wisdom. May you be blessed by my devotion to you.

How wise are you?

October 19

GRAVE CLOTHES REMOVED

When he had said this, Jesus called in a loud voice, "Lazarus, come out!" The dead man came out, his hands and feet wrapped with strips of linen, and a cloth around his face. Jesus said to them, "Take off the grave clothes and let him go" (John 11:43-44, NIV).

Amazing things happen when grave clothes are removed, Jesus. Thank you for removing mine. Help me to remember that I'm no longer bound by the things of the past. I have a new beginning in you.

How do Jesus' words resonate with you?

October 20

GOD WILL FIGHT

"The LORD your God is going with you! He will fight for you against your enemies, and he will give you victory!" (Deuteronomy 20:4, NLT)

Lord, when you are with me, impenetrable walls fall down.
Waters part. The enemy runs when no one chases. With you
all things are possible. You are the game changer.

Thank you for going with me.

Thank you for fighting for me.

Thank you for giving me victory.

I praise you for being my mighty God.

What "enemy" do you need victory over today?

October 21

HIS GREATNESS

How great is our Lord! His power is absolute!
His understanding is beyond comprehension! (Psalm 147:5, NLT)

Limitless Lord, I praise you for your greatness. You are omnipotent, omnipresent, and omniscient—the God who was, who is, and who is to come. You have not changed, nor do you plan to change. You are boundless, boundary-less, and infinitely beyond anything I can imagine.

You are love. You are life. You are light. You are creator. Sustainer. Provider. Helper. Giver. Fulfiller. Keeper. Redeemer. Multiplier. You are undeniable and incomprehensible.

I can't understand you, but I can know you. Because I know you, I can trust you. Thank you for all you do and all you are, Lord. May I honor you by believing that you're big enough to handle everything in my life.

How great is your God?

October 22

THE SPIRIT FROM GOD

No one can know a person's thoughts except that person's own spirit, and no one can know God's thoughts except God's own Spirit. And we have received God's Spirit (not the world's spirit), so we can know the wonderful things God has freely given us (1 Corinthians 2:11-12, NLT).

Thank you, God, for the wonderful presence of your Spirit, who helps me know what you've freely given me. I'm especially delighted that your Spirit welcomes me into your family and allows me the privilege of calling you Abba, my Father.

Because of your Spirit living within me, I have access to your wisdom, and I can see things from your perspective. I appreciate the insight, discernment, understanding, and revelation I receive.

The Spirit you've given me doesn't think or operate as the world does. He teaches me things that are far above the world's systems and values. He makes known your thoughts—including your thoughts about me—your secrets, and your truth. I'm grateful for all I've learned. I rejoice in the Spirit's work in my life, and I rejoice in you.

What things has the Spirit revealed to you about God?

October 23

A Lifetime God

"I will be your God throughout your lifetime—
until your hair is white with age.
I made you, and I will care for you.
I will carry you along and save you" (Isaiah 46:4, NLT).

I praise you, Lord, for being my lifetime God. You were with me years ago when I was hidden in my mother's womb. Even before I was born, you had a purpose and plan for me. Your desire was for me to love you and serve you all the days of my life, but you didn't force your will on me. Instead, you gently wooed me into a personal relationship with you.

Throughout the years, you've assured me of your constant presence, and I've been blessed by your goodness and care. You've never failed me. In your strength you've carried me when I had no strength of my own, and you've delivered me time and time again. I can count on you today, and I'll be able to count on you when my hair is white with age. I rejoice, Lord, that every day with you is sweeter than the day before.

How has your relationship with God changed
throughout your lifetime?

October 24

PROMISE KEEPER

Let us hold firmly to the hope that we have confessed, because we can
trust God to do what he promised (Hebrews 10:23, NCV).

What good is hope if it's in someone who breaks promises? How can I
trust a person who doesn't tell the truth? People always let me down,
Lord, but you never will. Because you are faithful to your Word and to
your divine character, I can hold unswervingly to the hope I profess.

I praise you for being dependable, and I thank you for your promises
that keep me going. My confidence rests in you.

If you became even more sure of God's faithfulness than you
are now, how would that affect your life?

October 25

He Carries My Cares

Cast your cares on the LORD
and he will sustain you;
he will never let
the righteous be shaken (Psalm 55:22, NIV).

Loving God, you invite me to cast my cares on you and promise that you'll sustain me. When I trust you with my troubles, you give me unshakable peace. I've experienced the way this works, and others have witnessed my calm spirit.

There's no problem too big, no mountain too tall, no storm too dark, and no sorrow too deep for you to handle. I know that to be true, Lord, and because you're always faithful, I should be able to easily place my burdens in your charge. Yet sometimes I cling more tightly to them than I do to you. I need help in letting go.

Lord, would you turn my thoughts to you and away from the things that weigh me down? Would you deepen my trust? I want you to be glorified in me and through me, and I want others to be intrigued by your presence at work in my life.

Which do you cling to more often—your troubles or the Lord?

October 26

THE LORD'S POWER

The LORD made the earth by his power,
and he preserves it by his wisdom.
With his own understanding
he stretched out the heavens.
When he speaks in the thunder,
the heavens roar with rain.
He causes the clouds to rise over the earth.
He sends the lightning with the rain
and releases the wind from his storehouses (Jeremiah 10:12-13, NLT).

I praise you for your power, Lord. With it you made the earth.

I praise you for your wisdom, Lord.
With it you preserve everything you made.

I praise you for your understanding, Lord.
With it you stretched out the vast heavens.

You speak in the thunder, and the heavens roar with rain. The clouds, lightning, and wind obey your commands. I worship you, Lord, for you are the blessed controller of all things.

As you meditate on these words, what thoughts
do you have about God?

October 27

Birth from God

To all who believed him and accepted him, he gave the right to become children of God. They are reborn—not with a physical birth resulting from human passion or plan, but a birth that comes from God (John 1:12-13, NLT).

What an incredible gift, Lord! The right to become your child. Wow! Your gift came at an extravagant price. In order for me to have the privilege of rebirth in you, Jesus had to take down death. Personally. Help me to never forget the high cost he paid or your extreme love that made it possible.

Thank you that all who welcome Jesus into their lives and trust in his name can claim the title "Child of God." Thank you for that special position and for all the benefits that come along with it. Thank you for the honor of calling you Father.

I praise you for being the perfect Father. You are faithful, trustworthy, generous, loving, kind, compassionate, caring, and good. And you are mine. I'm eternally grateful.

What significance does the title "Child of God" have for you?

October 28

MY WONDERFUL LORD

The Lord is righteous in everything he does;
he is filled with kindness.
The Lord is close to all who call on him,
yes, to all who call on him in truth.
He grants the desires of those who fear him;
he hears their cries for help and rescues them.
The Lord protects all those who love him,
but he destroys the wicked (Psalm 145:17-20, NLT).

Lord, you are righteous in everything you do, filled with kindness, close to all who call on you in truth, granter of desires of those who fear you, responder and rescuer for those who cry for help, protector of those who love you, and destroyer of the wicked.

Thank you for your presence in my life and for the ways you show your love and care. I'm in awe that you would want to be intimately involved with me. You're a great and wonderful God, and it's my honor to praise you, worship you, and live in relationship with you.

In your life, how has God shown himself
to be the things mentioned above?

October 29

NO PROBLEM WITH MOUNTAINS OR GATES

I will go before you
and will level the mountains;
I will break down gates of bronze
and cut through bars of iron (Isaiah 45:2, NIV).

Mighty God, although this was promised to another people at another time, I'm thankful that you are the same big God today. You are able to level mountains. You are able to break down gates of bronze. And you are able to cut through bars of iron. I praise you for being a God who is able.

There are no barriers to what you can do, God. Your power has no limits. Nothing can derail your purposes and plans in my life. Mountains and gates of bronze may slow down the process, but you go before me and make the way straight. I'm in awe of you, Lord.

What mountains does God need to level, and what gates
does he need to break down in your life?

October 30

GOD IS FOR US

If God is for us, who [can be] against us? [Who can be our foe,
if God is on our side?] (Romans 8:31b, AMP)

God, I celebrate the truth that you are for me, not against me.
You are on my side. With that knowledge, I have nothing to fear.
Thank you for the assurance that you are with me today and for the
many reminders that you will be with me tomorrow.

If you are for me, who could ever stop me? If you are with me,
what could stand against me? I'm grateful that the answers are
"no one" and "nothing." I praise you for being my God. In you I trust.
In your promises I rest.

How are you comforted in knowing that God is for you and
he's on your side?

October 31

No Reason for Fear

The Lord is my light and my salvation—
so why should I be afraid?
The Lord is my fortress, protecting me from danger,
so why should I tremble? (Psalm 27:1, NLT)

Lord, you are my light. You are my salvation.
There's no reason for me to be afraid.

You are my fortress. You protect me from danger.
There's no reason for me to be afraid.

Thank you that when the forces of darkness try to overtake me, I can
run to you and know I'm safe. There's no reason for me to be afraid.

What reasons do you have to fear?

November

He has shown kindness by giving you rain

from heaven and crops in their seasons;

he provides you with plenty of food

and fills your hearts with joy.

ACTS 14:17, NIV

November 1

LIGHT IN DARKNESS

His life is the light that shines through the darkness—and the
darkness can never extinguish it (John 1:5, TLB).

Jesus, I praise you for being my light. The darkness of oppression,
testing, trials, or sorrows can't overtake me when I put my trust in
you. Nothing can extinguish the effects of your being present and at
work in my life.

As I grow closer to you and you create in me a heart like yours,
people notice. They see the gleam in my eyes and the joy and peace
that radiates from me despite my circumstances. People are drawn
to the light within me, and that's you! Thank you for illuminating my
darkness and for using me to shine the light on you. You're the hope
this world needs.

In what dark situation do you need Jesus
to shine his light today?

November 2

UNFATHOMABLE LORD

Who can fathom the Spirit of the LORD,
or instruct the LORD as his counselor? (Isaiah 40:13, NIV)

I exalt your name, Lord, for you are unfathomable. You don't consult with experts for advice, because you are the source of wisdom. You don't seek guidance, because you are the Counselor. You don't refer to physicists, engineers, architects, biologists, or zoologists for design help, because you are the Creator.

You don't require instructions, because you are the Teacher of teachers. You don't need my opinions about how to handle my problems, because you hold my future and know what's best for my life. All the treasures of wisdom and knowledge are found in you. I praise you for having the answer to my every troubling situation, question, or need. I trust in you alone.

In what specific areas do you need God's wisdom,
answers, or counsel right now?

November 3

He Will Hear and Restore

"If my people who are called by my name will humble themselves and pray and seek my face and turn from their wicked ways, I will hear from heaven and will forgive their sins and restore their land" (2 Chronicles 7:14, NLT).

Lord, what a privilege it is to be called by your name! What an honor that you know my name! I praise you for being a relational God and for allowing me to know you—the King of the universe—in intimate ways.

God, my nation is on my heart. I'm concerned about the path we're on and the wicked ways of so many in leadership. Yet before I point my finger at others, I need to look at myself. When I do that I see pride, self-righteousness, judgmental thoughts, and my own wickedness. Forgive me.

My desires are that you would keep me humble and obedient. Keep me seeking your face, and then use me to draw others to you. Would you please restore my land? I know those are your desires as well, Lord. Thank you for hearing my prayers.

How do you interpret this promise?

November 4

A KINGDOM ETERNAL

Your kingdom is an everlasting kingdom,
and your dominion endures through all generations.
The LORD is trustworthy in all he promises
and faithful in all he does (Psalm 145:13, NIV).

I exalt you, Sovereign God, for you are the supreme power who has authority over every created being. Your kingdom is eternal and unshakable. I celebrate the fact that you'll never get voted out of office and that you will reign forever and ever! Hallelujah!

Because of the media, I receive daily reminders of the lies, deception, broken promises, moral failures, bad decisions, and poor leadership of our elected officials. How I praise you for being the one ruler who is trustworthy all the time! I praise you for being faithful, holy, and wise. You always do what you say, and you're gracious in everything you do.

I'm grateful that no matter what happens in this country or in this world, you are ultimately and forever in control. My hope is in you.

How does God's rule compare to that of our elected officials?

November 5

PLACE OF HIGHEST PRIVILEGE

Since we have been made right in God's sight by faith in his promises,
we can have real peace with him because of what Jesus Christ our
Lord has done for us. For because of our faith, he has brought us
into this place of highest privilege where we now stand, and we
confidently and joyfully look forward to actually becoming all that
God has had in mind for us to be (Romans 5:1-2, TLB).

God, thank you for your precious promises, and thank you that I've been made right in your sight because I believe in them. What a blessing that my sin no longer prevents me from having real peace with you. It's all because of what Jesus did for me! How I praise you for that radical act of love and kindness.

I now gratefully stand in grace—the place of highest privilege, the place of freedom and life transformation. I confidently and joyfully look forward to becoming all you want me to be, and doing all you want me to do for your honor and glory.

How will you thank God today for bringing you into the
place of highest privilege?

November 6

THE LIFTER OF MY HEAD

You, O Lord, are a shield around me;
you are my glory, the one who holds my head high (Psalm 3:3, NLT).

Oh Lord, I praise you for you are my glory, the one who holds my head high. When my spirit is downcast, when I cower in fear or shame, when I feel downtrodden, when it seems my circumstances have taken a downward turn, you place your hand under my chin and gently lift up my head, toward you.

As my eyes are on you, you remind me of your love. You remind me of important truths. You remind me of who you are. You remind me that you are a shield around me. Nothing can penetrate your shield when I'm looking at you. Nothing can harm me: not thoughts, not circumstances, not people, not evil. Guard my heart, Lord. Guard my mind. And keep my eyes on you. I want my shield of faith to stay permanently in place.

How is God the lifter of your head?

November 7

SPIRIT OF TRUTH

"When the Spirit of truth comes, he will guide you into all truth.
He will not speak on his own but will tell you what he has heard.
He will tell you about the future. He will bring me glory by telling
you whatever he receives from me. All that belongs to the Father
is mine; this is why I said, 'The Spirit will tell you whatever
he receives from me'" (John 16:13-15, NLT).

Holy Spirit, I rejoice in your presence within me. Thank you for keeping me connected with the Father and for guiding me into all truth. I'm delighted that I'm not left to wander aimlessly or to flounder on my own. You direct me in God's purposes and reveal to me his plans.

You are a live-in, love-filled, patient guide—an incredible gift! I praise you for your work in my life. May I honor you by staying tuned in to your voice.

How has the Spirit of truth worked in your life?

November 8

WEEPING AND JOY

For his anger lasts only a moment,
but his favor lasts a lifetime!
Weeping may last through the night,
but joy comes with the morning (Psalm 30:5, NLT).

Lord, I praise you, for you are compassionate and gracious, slow to anger, abounding in love. I'm grateful that your anger lasts only a moment, and I'm blessed that the favor you shower on me lasts a lifetime. Thank you for your encouraging reminder that your favor is forever, and weeping is not. I have days when it seems as if the grief will never end. But it will pass. Eventually.

I'm comforted with the knowledge that my weeping is not insignificant to you. You keep track of all my sorrows. You collect all my tears in your bottle and record each one in your book.
You wrap your loving arms around me and hold me close.
Thank you for meeting me in my pain and heartache and walking through it with me. In your presence is fullness of joy.
And in your presence, the weeping will end. Eventually.

What hope do these words hold for you?

November 9

HE GIVES VICTORY

"Do not be afraid of them," the LORD *said to Joshua,*
"for I have given you victory over them. Not a single one
of them will be able to stand up to you" (Joshua 10:8, NLT).

God, you are amazing in the way you work! I praise you for your creative imagination and the unconventional methods you use for winning battles. Through the element of surprise, confusion of the enemy camp, hailstones, and the sun standing still, you gave Joshua and his army a great win. But what stands out to me most is that you told Joshua, even before he engaged in the conflict, that you *had given* him victory over the opposition. He had already won!

When I trust in you, you give me victory beforehand as well. I'm strong and courageous. Without fear. And I have peace because I'm reminded of your presence. Trust is where the ultimate victory is won, well before the physical battle is played out. Thank you that in spite of the external outcome, I'm triumphant when I'm in your hands and in your will. That's what I call an unconventional method!

When have you experienced victory ahead of the battle?

November 10

ENGRAVED ON HIS PALMS

"Can a mother forget the baby at her breast
and have no compassion on the child she has borne?
Though she may forget,
I will not forget you!
See, I have engraved you on the palms of my hands"
(Isaiah 49:15-16, NIV).

Lord Jesus, how can I express the overwhelming emotions I have as I ponder these words? You will never forsake me. You will never forget me. You have a constant reminder of me on the palms of your hands. My name is engraved there, right next to the nail scars.

I'm humbled. I'm in awe. I'm eternally grateful.

As you ponder these words, what feelings do they evoke?

November 11

PROTECTION OF ANGELS

He will order his angels
to protect you wherever you go.
They will hold you up with their hands
so you won't even hurt your foot on a stone (Psalm 91:11-12, NLT).

Almighty God, I'm comforted in knowing that because I love you and acknowledge you, you've commanded your angels to watch over me. They're with me wherever I go. I praise you for caring about my protection.

Thank you for positioning your ministering spirits and heavenly warriors around me. Thank you for the many special earthly servants you assign to do your bidding in my life. May I always be mindful of their work on my behalf, and may I gratefully remember that you're the one who sent them.

What comfort do you receive in knowing that God has assigned his angels to watch over you?

November 12

FOUNTAIN OF SALVATION

With joy you will drink deeply
from the fountain of salvation! (Isaiah 12:3, NLT)

Jesus, I praise you because you are the inexhaustible fountain of salvation. Like the immense satisfaction I receive when taking a long, cool drink after baking in the blazing sun, you are refreshment for my parched soul. The more I drink of you, the closer I'm drawn to your heart. The deeper I go, the more I live in your abundance and the more I have to share with those around me.

Fill my cup, Lord. Help me to live each day in the rich blessings of your salvation.

How thirsty are you?

November 13

THE GOD WHO SEES ME

She gave this name to the LORD who spoke to her: "You are the God
who sees me," for she said, "I have now seen the One who sees me"
(Genesis 16:13, NIV).

Oh Lord, I praise you for being El-roi, the God who sees me. As
you saw Hagar in her misery—scorned by her mistress, thrown out,
all alone, and thinking she was going to die in the desert—you
see what's happening in my life, and you're with me. You see my
disappointments and successes. You see my dreams shattered and
fulfilled. You see my tears and my laughter, my fears and my hopes,
my battles and my triumphs.

I'm blessed that your all-seeing eyes are upon me each moment of
every day. Help me to remember that despite how the situation looks,
and despite how I feel, you are present and you care.

When do you have trouble believing that God sees you?

November 14

The word of the LORD holds true,
and we can trust everything he does (Psalm 33:4, NLT).

How can I trust a liar, Lord? How can I trust someone whose intent is to deceive? How can I trust people whose integrity has been compromised? If their word is no good, what about them is? I dislike the feeling of distrust, and I dislike being suspect of anything those who have broken my trust do. It grieves me deeply and fills my insides with turmoil. The relationship is hard to mend.

With you I'll never need to face that issue. Every word of yours holds true. I can trust everything you do. I don't have to wonder whether you'll keep your promises because you never speak empty words. Thank you, Lord! You are always worthy of my trust. You are always faithful. You are always true. You are always you. I praise you for being my trustworthy God. I can rest in you.

Why is being able to trust God's Word important?

November 15

THE LORD'S ARM AND EAR

Surely the arm of the LORD is not too short to save,
nor his ear too dull to hear (Isaiah 59:1, NIV).

Surely your arm is not too short to save, Lord. Surely your ear is not too dull to hear. Why? You have no limitations! No one is out of your reach. Nothing is beyond your ability to handle.

Your outstretched arm is ready to minister to my every need. Your attentive ear hears my every cry for help. Thank you for being my strong and powerful, caring God. You're worthy of my praise.

How does this reminder give you hope?

November 16

JESUS HEALS ALL

A vast crowd brought to him people who were lame, blind, crippled,
those who couldn't speak, and many others. They laid them before
Jesus, and he healed them all. The crowd was amazed! Those who
hadn't been able to speak were talking, the crippled were made well,
the lame were walking, and the blind could see again! And they
praised the God of Israel (Matthew 15:30-31, NLT).

Lord, you have all power and all wisdom. I praise you because no
physical, spiritual, mental, or emotional problem is beyond your reach.
I praise you, too, for having purposes and plans for each of your
children. Sometimes those purposes and plans involve healing your
children for your glory. Other times you receive glory through filling
them with your grace.

Thank you for having good plans for my life, Lord. With whatever
you do in me or for me, I want the crowds to be amazed.
Use me to shine the light on you in big ways so people
will see your work and praise your name.

What work has God done in you to bring glory to his name?

November 17

He Hears and Gives

We are confident that he hears us whenever we ask for anything
that pleases him. And since we know he hears us when we make our
requests, we also know that he will give us what we ask for
(1 John 5:14-15, NLT).

I praise you, loving Father, for being such a faithful God. Because
you've proven yourself so many times, I can have confidence in you
and the way you work. I'm grateful that you allow me to come boldly
before you. What a privilege! Thank you for giving me your full
attention and for hearing my requests.

As I draw closer to you and seek to live in accordance with your will,
you reveal to me the things that please you. I know that if I ask for
anything within your desires for my life, you delight in giving it to me.
You bless me, Lord. May I honor you with my requests.

What requests are you currently making to God?

November 18

THE LORD IS KING

The LORD is king! He is robed in majesty.
Indeed, the LORD is robed in majesty and armed with strength.
The world stands firm
and cannot be shaken (Psalm 93:1, NLT).

You, oh Lord, are most high over all the earth. You are exalted far above all gods. You are my King, and I worship your majesty. Unto you be all glory, honor, and praise! The world is in your hands and under your sovereign rule. It can't be shaken nor can you. Your throne was established long ago; your dominion is eternal.

I'm humbled and grateful to be subjected to your authority. Because you're my King, I have the best care possible. I'm safe and secure under your supervision, and all my needs are met. You're powerful, strong, and just, and you extend your grace and goodness toward me. I revere your holy and great name. May your kingdom come and your will be done on earth as it is in heaven.

How will you show honor to your King today?

November 19

CHILDREN AND HEIRS

All who are led by the Spirit of God are children of God. So you have
not received a spirit that makes you fearful slaves. Instead,
you received God's Spirit when he adopted you as his own children.
Now we call him, "Abba, Father." For his Spirit joins with our spirit to
affirm that we are God's children. And since we are his children, we
are his heirs. In fact, together with Christ we are heirs of God's glory.
But if we are to share his glory, we must also share his suffering
(Romans 8:14-17, NLT).

I'm yours, Lord! How I praise you for adopting me as your child!
I rejoice in the privilege of calling you Abba, Father.

Thank you for the way your Spirit connects with my spirit and affirms
that I belong to you. Thank you for making me an heir and for the
many riches and blessings I experience through my relationship with
you. Thank you for the suffering I face because I'm yours; I don't
enjoy it, but you use it for my good and your glory. I love you!

What part of being God's child do you most appreciate?

November 20

JESUS GIVES VISION

When Jesus came to the place where they were, he stopped in the road
and called, "What do you want me to do for you?"
"Sir," they said, "we want to see!"
Jesus was moved with pity for them and touched their eyes. And
instantly they could see, and followed him (Matthew 20:32-34, TLB).

Touch my eyes, Jesus. I want to see things the way you see them. Help me to see myself not as a disobedient failure but as a forgiven child. Help me to see my unattainable mountains as journeys into new, richer heights of knowing you.

Help me to see roadblocks and interruptions as opportunities for you to work. Help me to see the thunderstorms of life as showers of blessing. Help me to see others as people you love. Help me to see truth. Help me to see you. Be my vision, Lord.

What do you want to see?

November 21

NUMBERS AND NAMES

He counts the stars
and calls them all by name (Psalm 147:4, NLT).

Lord, you're an awesome and amazing God! I have a hard time remembering the names of my loved ones, yet you count the stars and call them all by name! Not only do you know how many stars you personally hung in the sky, but you also know how many grains of sand are on the shore and the number of hairs on my head.

Thank you for another reminder that nothing is impossible for you. It means that you can handle my big prayers. I praise you for being a big God!

If you could fully grasp that nothing is impossible for God,
what big prayer request would you bring to him?

November 22

Keep your eyes on Jesus, our leader and instructor. He was willing to die a shameful death on the cross because of the joy he knew would be his afterwards; and now he sits in the place of honor by the throne of God. If you want to keep from becoming fainthearted and weary, think about his patience as sinful men did such terrible things to him (Hebrews 12:2-3, TLB).

Jesus, you're my leader and instructor, the author and perfecter of my faith. I praise you for what you did on my behalf! You were willing to die a shameful death so that I could have a right relationship with your Father. And what great joy you had when your mission was complete!

Thank you for not growing weary or fainthearted, even as you endured such horrible opposition. Thank you for not giving up. Because of you, I have hope and life and intimate communion with my God. Help me to keep my eyes on you through good times and bad, and help me to learn from your example. I want my life to please you.

What do you learn when your eyes are on Jesus?

November 23

FROM EVERLASTING TO EVERLASTING

Before the mountains were born
or you brought forth the whole world,
from everlasting to everlasting you are God (Psalm 90:2, NIV).

Lord, I praise you for being my everlasting-to-everlasting God. You are the high and exalted one who lives forever. In the beginning you created the heavens and the earth, yet you yourself have no beginning or creator. You're self-existent, self-sufficient, and without limitation. You're not bound by time or space.

These are deep truths, Lord, and I lack the power to comprehend them. But if I understood everything about you, you wouldn't be God, and I wouldn't need you. Despite them being confusing and unexplainable, I do grasp the rich significance of what they mean for me: Because you're eternal, your blessings to your loved ones are eternal as well. Thank you! I look forward to entering fully into the eternal life I already possess in Christ, and basking in the joy of your presence forever.

How does God's everlasting nature impact you?

November 24

JESUS SEES AND KNOWS ME

"How do you know me?" Nathanael asked.
Jesus answered, "I saw you while you were still under the fig tree
before Philip called you" (John 1:48, NIV).

Jesus, I praise you for being my omnipresent Lord. You see all and you know all. From a distance, you saw Nathanael under the fig tree. He didn't know you, but you knew him, and you knew exactly what he needed. You answered his questions, revealed yourself to him in conversation, and brought him into a relationship with you.

Likewise, before I knew you, you knew me. You saw me. You loved me. You wooed me to you. I've had the joy of getting to know you in personal ways ever since. I'm grateful that I'm not hidden from you. I'm blessed that you're in my life. I'm amazed by your attention. I worship and adore you, sweet Jesus! You're precious to me.

What comfort do you receive in knowing that you're not
hidden from Jesus?

November 25

BREAD AND WATER

Then Jesus declared, "I am the bread of life. Whoever comes to me
will never go hungry, and whoever believes in me will never be thirsty"
(John 6:35, NIV).

Jesus, I praise you for being the bread of life and living water. Just
as you provided manna and water in the desert to physically sustain
the Israelites, you are the sustenance my soul needs. Only you can
truly satisfy my hunger and quench my thirst. I can't live without you.
Because I partake of what you offer me, I'll never have to die.

Your bread and water diet is perfect for me, Jesus. It doesn't grow
old. I celebrate the fact that when I supersize my meals they work for
me instead of against me. The more I consume, the better I look. The
more I consume, the better I feel. The more I consume, the healthier
and stronger I become. I love that program! I love what you do
for me! I've tasted and I've seen that you are good. Thank you for
keeping me well fed.

What do you think of Jesus' bread and water diet?

November 26

THE LORD IS GOOD

Enter his gates with thanksgiving
and his courts with praise;
give thanks to him and praise his name.
For the LORD is good and his love endures forever;
his faithfulness continues through all generations
(Psalm 100:4-5, NIV).

How I love you, Lord! How grateful I am to be your child! Thank you for your goodness and faithfulness. Thank you for being my God. Thank you for loving me and desiring a relationship with me. Thank you for your generosity. Thank you for your presence, power, and provision. Thank you for being my rock, my refuge, my stronghold, my deliverer, my safe place, my haven of rest, my strong tower, my supply, my love, my life, my all-in-all, my Abba, my God in whom I trust.

Thank you for the purpose and plan you have for me. Thank you for having answers to my questions. Thank you for putting things in place for my future. Thank you for blessing my life through the relationships I have. Thank you for innumerable reasons to praise your name. It's my joy to honor you.

For how many things can you thank God today?

November 27

EVERYTHING COMES FROM HIM

Who am I, and who are my people, that we could give anything to you? Everything we have has come from you, and we give you only what you first gave us! (1 Chronicles 29:14, NLT)

What can I give you that you haven't already given me, Lord? Everything I have, I owe to you. You pour out your goodness and abundance on my life every day. Your blessings never stop. May I daily acknowledge your generosity and offer you the gift of a grateful heart.

What can you offer God to show your appreciation for all he's given to you?

November 28

MY STRENGTH

I love you, LORD;
you are my strength (Psalm 18:1, NLT).

I love you, Lord, and I praise you for being my strength.
When I'm weak and up against impossible circumstances,
when I'm near the brink of breakdown, when I have no internal
fortitude left, when I don't know how I will carry on, I cry out to you.

Thank you for listening to my outbursts. Thank you for catching my
tears. Thank you for holding me in your embrace of grace. Thank
you for reminding me of truth. Thank you for assuring me of your
presence. Thank you for stabilizing my shaky legs and trembling heart.
Because of you I can endure. I trust in you and I am helped.

For what situation do you need God's strength today?

November 29

HE ANSWERS ME

When I called, you answered me;
you greatly emboldened me (Psalm 138:3, NIV).

Lord, when I call, you answer. Thank you for hearing every cry of my heart. I know you'll respond whether the issues are big or small. I'm in awe that you—the God of the universe—make time for me and care about what's going on in my life. When I call, you assure me of your presence, and I have courage and confidence to face whatever situation is before me.

When I call, you remind me of who you are, how much you love me, and that there's nothing you cannot do. That emboldens me. I praise you for being my always accessible, attentive, and gracious God. I'm grateful for the privilege of relationship with you.

How are you emboldened when you call out to God?

November 30

Always God

From eternity to eternity I am God. No one can oppose what I do
(Isaiah 43:13, TLB).

Yes, Lord, you are God, and how grateful I am that you're my God!
I worship you because you've always been and will always be God.
There's never been a time when you weren't God. I praise you for
never changing. I praise you for being I AM.

No matter what the world's distinguished professors, celebrated
scientists, famous Hollywood stars, or illustrious leaders say or do to
prove otherwise, you will always exist. You will always reign. You will
always be in control. You will always direct the course of world affairs.
You will always love. You will always keep your promises. You will
always be true. You will always have a plan. You will always deserve
all honor and glory and praise. God, I love you. May you always be on
the throne of my heart.

Why is it important to understand that God
has always been God?

December

"It is finished! I am the Alpha and the Omega—

the Beginning and the End. To all who are

thirsty I will give freely from the springs.

of the water of life"

Revelation 21:6, NLT

December 1

PROTECTION AND POWER

The LORD is my rock, my fortress, and my savior;
my God is my rock, in whom I find protection.
He is my shield, the power that saves me,
and my place of safety (Psalm 18:2, NLT).

I worship you, God—my rock, my fortress, my savior. You're my hope.
When fears pursue me, I run to you and I'm safe; I cannot be shaken.
I praise you for being my solid, immovable rock. My protection. You
hide me in your clefts where the cares of the world can't touch me.
You shelter me from high winds and cover me in stormy weather.
I'm at peace when I'm in your presence.

Your faithfulness is my shield. You're the power that saves me and
my place of safety. I'm secure in you. I love you, Lord—my refuge and
strength. You're a very present help in times of trouble.

In what ways does God protect you and save you?

December 2

CREATOR OF NIGHT SKIES

Lift up your eyes and look to the heavens:
Who created all these?
He who brings out the starry host one by one
and calls forth each of them by name.
Because of his great power and mighty strength,
not one of them is missing (Isaiah 40:26, NIV).

God, you have no equal. You're the everlasting God, the creator
of the ends of the earth. You don't grow tired or weary. But I do.
When I have days that I don't know how I'll endure because of the
trials, heartaches, or busyness of life, would you lift my head toward
heaven? As my eyes are focused upward, I'll see your handiwork
and remember that you're unchangeable, reliable, faithful, creative,
powerful, strong, and wise. And then I'll remember that you know me,
you love me, you care about me, and you're with me. My hope will be
reignited, and my strength renewed.

Thank you for the night skies, Lord, and thank you for all the
countless other reminders of your presence around me.
May they help me keep my eyes on you.

What special reminders do you have of God's presence?

December 3

THE WORD

In the beginning the Word already existed. The Word was with God,
and the Word was God. He existed in the beginning with God
(John 1:1-2, NLT).

I worship you, Jesus, and I exalt you as the eternal, all-powerful, living
Word of God. You are the alpha and omega, the first and the last, the
beginning and the end. I praise you for humbling yourself and coming
to earth, fully man and fully God. You came to reveal the Father to us
and to redeem all who believe and trust in you as Savior.

As the Word, you are the Father's spokesperson. You have all authority
and creative power. In the beginning, you spoke and everything
came into being. You spoke, and all creation had a time and place.
Throughout history and today, your Word accomplishes what you
desire and achieves your good purposes.

I rejoice that as the Word, you're present tense. I AM. You're always
present and always sufficient. You're all I need for my today and every
day. Those are the best words I could ever know. I praise you, Jesus!

What are some of your favorite words Jesus has spoken,
and why?

December 4

VISIBLE IMAGE OF INVISIBLE GOD

Christ is the visible image of the invisible God. He existed before
anything was created and is supreme over all creation, for through
him God created everything in the heavenly realms and on earth.
He made the things we can see and the things we can't see—such
as thrones, kingdoms, rulers, and authorities in the unseen world.
Everything was created through him and for him
(Colossians 1:15-16, NLT).

Jesus, when I think about who you are, I scarce can take it in.
>   You are the visible image of the invisible God.
>   You are the exact and perfect representation of God.
>   You are the revelation of God.
>   You embody God.
>   You possess all the elements and attributes of God's nature.
>   You existed before anything was created.
>   You are supreme over all creation.
>   Through you all things were created.
>   You have all authority and power.
>   You are the King of kings and have the name above all names.

And you humbled yourself to be born in a manger.

I scarce can take it in.

How does your mind process this incredible truth?

December 5

WAY, TRUTH, LIFE

Jesus told him, "I am the way, the truth, and the life. No one can come to the Father except through me" (John 14:6, NLT).

I praise you, Jesus, because you bridged the gap between the most high, holy God and unholy me. You, and you alone, made it possible for me to have a personal relationship with your Father. I'm grateful every day for your incredible gift that came at an extraordinary price—your life. Though many imposters claim to be a way, you are the only way.

I praise you for being the source of truth. Truth helps me overpower the lying deceiver, and he hates that! Thank you for the gift of your powerful Word and the help of your Spirit, who guides me into all truth. May I always keep your words in my mind and on my heart.

I praise you for being the life. You created life and give new life. Because you conquered death, I'm blessed to experience full life and forever life in you. You are the way, truth, and life, Jesus, and you deserve all my worship and praise.

How will you praise the way, truth, and life today?

December 6

WONDER AND AWE

Jesus knew what they were thinking, so he asked them, "Why do you question this in your hearts? Is it easier to say 'Your sins are forgiven,' or 'Stand up and walk'? So I will prove to you that the Son of Man has the authority on earth to forgive sins." Then Jesus turned to the paralyzed man and said, "Stand up, pick up your mat, and go home!" And immediately, as everyone watched, the man jumped up, picked up his mat, and went home praising God. Everyone was gripped with great wonder and awe, and they praised God, exclaiming, "We have seen amazing things today!" (Luke 5:22-26, NLT)

Jesus, I praise you for being a wonderful and awesome God. You know what's on people's minds, you know their spiritual and physical needs, and you have the ability to care for them. You have authority to forgive sins, and you make it possible. You have power to heal and to conquer death.

Thank you for the amazing things you have done, and plan to do, in my life. I rejoice in who you are!

How has Jesus shown his authority and power in your life?

December 7

His Guidance

By day the LORD went ahead of them in a pillar of cloud to guide them on their way and by night in a pillar of fire to give them light, so that they could travel by day or night. Neither the pillar of cloud by day nor the pillar of fire by night left its place in front of the people (Exodus 13:21-22, NIV).

God, I thank you for the way you guide your children and assure them of your presence. Just as your presence was obvious to Moses and the Israelites many years ago, you're with me today. I don't have the cloud as they did, but I have the gift of your Spirit within me and the gift of your Word to provide light on my journey.

I praise you for the Spirit of truth who accompanies me at all times. When I listen to him, he shows me your ways and teaches me your paths. I'm grateful that in the times I don't know what to do, you're faithful to guide and enlighten me as I wait on you.

How has God guided and enlightened you lately?

December 8

No Other Name

There is salvation in no one else! God has given no other name under heaven by which we must be saved (Acts 4:12, NLT).

Jesus, I give praise to your name because you're the author of my salvation. Yours is the only name under heaven that has authority to save. You're the way, the truth, and the life. No one comes to the Father except through you. Thank you for being my Savior. Your name is powerful. It unlocks shackles, opens the floodgates of heaven, and transforms lives. But how will people call on you for salvation unless they've heard about you first?

Would you use me to shine the light on you, Jesus? I want you to be exalted and glorified in my life. I want to live in such a way that people are curious about you. Equip me with your truth and empower me by your Spirit so I'll always have an answer for those who want to know about the hope I have. May I honor your name by sharing it with others, and may you look down on me and smile.

With whom can you share the name of Jesus?

December 9

Gifts from Above

Every good and perfect gift is from above, coming down
from the Father of the heavenly lights, who does not change
like shifting shadows (James 1:17, NIV).

I delight in you, Father, and I praise you for not changing. I can rely on your love every day of my life. Thank you for the way you shower abundant blessings on me. You're my generous and kind-hearted God. In this crazy season of gift giving, would you help me remember that every good and perfect gift comes from you? This world offers nothing comparable. The only things that truly satisfy are from your hands.

Help me to not neglect your gifts, Lord. I want to acknowledge all you've given, and I want to gratefully receive all you have for me. May my enjoyment of your generosity bring you pleasure.

What good and perfect gifts has the Father given you?

December 10

A BIG GIVER

Since he did not spare even his own Son but gave him up for us all,
won't he also give us everything else? (Romans 8:32, NLT)

Father, I love you. I worship and adore you. May your name be
glorified in all the earth. You're a wonderful, merciful God who cares
deeply for his children and knows exactly what we need. I praise you
for your giving nature and for your extraordinary generosity. Every
good and perfect gift comes from you, God. And the biggest and best
you ever gave was Jesus. You sent him to earth to die so we might
have life. It's a gift that will be celebrated throughout eternity.

Since you did not spare even your own Son but gave him up for us
all, doesn't it just make sense that you would give us everything else
we need? Nothing is too big for you to accomplish, and nothing is
too small for your attention. Help me to remember those important
truths as I pray. May I honor you by bringing all my needs, and even
my desires, to you in prayer.

How does bringing all our needs and desires to God honor him?

December 11

THE SHEPHERD

"I am the good shepherd; I know my own sheep, and they know me"
(John 10:14, NLT).

Jesus, I praise you for being the good shepherd. You know your own sheep and they know you. You're a tender, compassionate shepherd who lovingly cares for your flock. You knew their greatest need was a Savior, so you willingly lay down your life. What a beautiful offering on their behalf.

As one of your little lambs, I can never praise you enough. May I always be grateful and mindful of what you did for me. It's the perfect gift.

How has the good shepherd's gift changed
the course of your life?

December 12

His Sheep

"My sheep listen to my voice; I know them, and they follow me"
(John 10:27, NLT).

As you lay in the manger, and the sheep roamed about, did they recognize your cry, Jesus? Did they want to linger at your feet? Did they know you were the good shepherd? I have a feeling they did. After all, you were the one who created them, and you have a distinctive voice.

I was the reason you were in that manger, Jesus, and now I'm blessed to be one of your precious lambs. I bow at your feet in adoration. The more I linger with you, the more I learn from you and become familiar with your voice. That's important for me to do, Lord, because there are too many voices in the world vying for my attention. Yours is the one that speaks truth. It's the one I want to discern.

Good Shepherd, would you keep me close to you? I want to follow you all the days of my life and bring glory to your name.

How are you able to recognize the good shepherd's voice?

December 13

Be Still

"Be still, and know that I am God;
I will be exalted among the nations,
I will be exalted in the earth" (Psalm 46:10, NIV).

Lord, this is a message you keep giving me. You want it to sink in.
Be still.
And know I AM.

I praise you for knowing just what I need, and I thank you for your
gentle reminders that nudge me to pay attention to you. May I AM be
exalted among the nations. May I AM be exalted in the earth.
And may I AM be exalted in me. I love you, Lord.

How does this verse speak to you today?

December 14

PROMISES KEPT

*The LORD kept his word and did for Sarah exactly what he had
promised (Genesis 21:1, NLT).*

Almighty God, I praise you for being a God who makes big promises,
and I praise you for being a God who keeps big promises. I'm grateful
for how those promises affect me. You made a special covenant with
Abraham thousands of years ago. You told him he'd become a great
nation and that all peoples on earth would be blessed through him.
That was an incredible promise for an old man with a barren wife.
"Nothing is impossible," you reminded them. And you kept your word!
Isaac was born to a 90-year-old woman and a 100-year-old man.

Hundreds of years later you told Isaac's descendant Mary that she
would give birth to a son and that she was to give him the name
Jesus. That was an incredible promise for a young virgin. "Nothing is
impossible," you reminded her. And you kept your word! The Son of
the most high was born, and all peoples on earth are blessed through
him. Lord, have I told you lately how amazing you are?

What are your thoughts right now?

December 15

MACRO-GOD AND MICRO-ME

When I look up into the night skies and see the work of your fingers—
the moon and the stars you have made—I cannot understand how you
can bother with mere puny man, to pay any attention to him!
(Psalm 8:3-4, TLB)

The heavens declare your glory, Lord. The skies proclaim the work of
your hands. You are amazing, God, and your universe proves it.
I think about the magi from the East, who many years ago looked
up at your macro-skies and handmade sky-jewelry and observed a
dazzling display of splendor. A stunning bright light you personally
placed there guided them to their Savior. My Savior.

As I lift up my eyes to those same skies and stars, and gaze at your
magnificent handiwork, I realize how small I am in comparison to you.
Why do you bother with me, Lord? Why do you take a second look my
way? And as I wonder, I hear you say, "Because I love you, that's why."
I'm humbled by your love, Lord, and I exalt your wonderful name.

What do you think about when you gaze at God's heavens?

December 16

EMMANUEL

Behold, the virgin shall become pregnant and give birth to a Son, and
they shall call His name Emmanuel—which, when translated, means,
God with us (Matthew 1:23, AMP).

I worship you, Jesus, my Emmanuel, and I praise you for the big way
your name impacts my life. "God with us." You came with an important
mission—a mission born out of love—and you willingly left your glory in
heaven to be born as a babe on earth. You walked among your people,
taught us how to live, and then died so we could truly live.

But you didn't leave us to stumble along on our own. Your Spirit is
now among us and dwells with any who believe in you. You're here
with me, Lord. I'll never have to face life alone. You see all,
you know all, and you care.

What does the name Emmanuel mean to you?

December 17

JESUS

The angel said to her, "Do not be afraid, Mary; you have found favor with God. You will conceive and give birth to a son, and you are to call him Jesus. He will be great and will be called the Son of the Most High. The Lord God will give him the throne of his father David, and he will reign over Jacob's descendants forever; his kingdom will never end" (Luke 1:30-33, NIV).

"Bless the Lord, oh my soul: and all that is within me, bless his holy name" (Psalm 103:1, KJV). I bless your name, Jesus, Son of the most high God. I worship you and honor you, for you are great and greatly to be praised. You are the King whose reign never ends.
I'm grateful you're mine.

Your name is the name above all other names and should be revered by all. I bow before you in humble adoration today, and I look forward to doing it throughout eternity. Jesus. What a beautiful name. What a beautiful Savior. I love you.

How will you show adoration and praise to Jesus today?

December 18

WONDERFUL COUNSELOR

For to us a child is born,
to us a son is given,
and the government will be on his shoulders.
And he will be called
Wonderful Counselor*, Mighty God,*
Everlasting Father, Prince of Peace (Isaiah 9:6, NIV, emphasis added).

Jesus, I praise your name for you are wonderful in counsel and excellent in wisdom. No other counselor can compare. You search me and know me. You can discern my thoughts from afar. You're able to sympathize with my weaknesses. Because you understand everything about me, you know exactly what I need.

You love me and have good plans for my life; therefore, I can trust all your advice. Thank you for the guidance you give. When I listen to you, you instruct me in the right course of action. It's not necessary for me to comprehend everything. I have no reason for anxiety because you graciously welcome me to discuss my concerns at any time with you. I'm grateful for your attentiveness and care. Wonderful Counselor, I worship you. I'm blessed by your presence in my life.

How is Jesus your wonderful counselor?

December 19

MIGHTY GOD

For to us a child is born,
to us a son is given,
and the government will be on his shoulders.
And he will be called
*Wonderful Counselor, **Mighty God**,*
Everlasting Father, Prince of Peace (Isaiah 9:6, NIV, emphasis added).

Jesus, I lift your name on high, for you are the mighty God, the master of everything. You are my limitless, uncontainable, unmovable, unshakable, undeniable, irrepressible, immeasurable, all-powerful, incomparable, nothing-is-too-hard-for-you, off-the-charts God. I'm in awe that you would want anything to do with me.

Thank you for wanting a relationship with me. Thank you for wanting to do big things in me, with me, and for me. I'm honored to call you my God.

How has Jesus proven himself to be a
mighty God in your life?

December 20

EVERLASTING FATHER

For to us a child is born,
to us a son is given,
and the government will be on his shoulders.
And he will be called
Wonderful Counselor, Mighty God,
Everlasting Father, *Prince of Peace (Isaiah 9:6, NIV, emphasis added).*

Jesus, I worship you as the Father of eternity. You're the creator of my life and the reason I look forward to a forever life with you. Thank you for your mercy and grace, your unconditional love and forgiveness. Though I don't deserve any of it, I rejoice in your good gifts.

I praise you for being faithful. When I need help, you're there. When I have a problem, you're there. When I need someone to wipe my tears, you're there. Because you're trustworthy, I can believe anything you say. I may not always understand, but I know your words are true. You're my provider, my rock, my shelter, my renewer of strength. I never run out of good things to say about you.

Everlasting Father, I praise you for the many ways you care for me. May I honor you with my trust and obedience all the days of my life.

What is the everlasting Father to you?

December 21

Prince of Peace

For to us a child is born,
to us a son is given,
and the government will be on his shoulders.
And he will be called
Wonderful Counselor, Mighty God,
*Everlasting Father, **Prince of Peace** (Isaiah 9:6, NIV, emphasis added).*

I praise you for your wonderful gift of peace, Jesus! I need it. The world needs it. And it's readily available through you. You didn't promise a trouble-free existence. You didn't promise perfect circumstances. But because you didn't want your children in turmoil or full of fear, you promised your peace. It's a peace that's accessible despite what's going on, and it comes from living in the light of your presence and trusting you.

I'm grateful, Jesus, but I'm even more grateful for how you as the prince of peace made possible my peaceful relationship with Almighty God, the Father. Because of the robe of righteousness you provided for me, my sin no longer gets in the way. I'm eternally blessed for such a beautiful gift. Thank you for your work in my life.

What's going on in your life right now where you
could use the help of the prince of peace?

December 22

SAVIOR

She will have a Son, and you shall name him Jesus (meaning 'Savior'),
for he will save his people from their sins (Matthew 1:21, TLB).

Precious Jesus, I bow before you in adoration. You're the mighty King,
ruler of everything. The hope of earth and joy of heaven. I'm honored
to love and worship you. I exalt your wonderful name, Jesus. It's
strong, it's powerful, and it carries a promise to save.

Thank you for keeping your promise. I praise you for being my Savior.

How will you honor the Savior today?

December 23

THE MESSIAH

The woman said, "I know the Messiah is coming—the one who is
called Christ. When he comes, he will explain everything to us."
Then Jesus told her, "I AM the Messiah!" (John 4:25-26, NLT)

I exalt you, Jesus, for you are the Messiah—the Lord's anointed one.
How I praise you that we're not still waiting for you to come! You're
here and you're at work in a big way. I need you, Jesus, because life is
messy. I'm so grateful to have a Savior I can lean on when I feel as if
I'm falling apart. You're my peace during times of distress, my strength
when I'm weak, my joy when I'm brokenhearted, the answer to my
questions. I can trust you to carry my load.

I worship you because you are I AM. I can take the "it is what it is"
parts of my life and put them in the hands of I AM THAT I AM and
know everything will be okay. You bless me, Jesus. Thank you for
being my Messiah.

Why do you need a Messiah?

December 24

HE CAME DOWN

The LORD said, "I have indeed seen the misery of my people in Egypt.
I have heard them crying out because of their slave drivers, and I am
concerned about their suffering. So I have come down to rescue them
from the hand of the Egyptians and to bring them up out of that land
into a good and spacious land, a land flowing with milk and honey"
(Exodus 3:7-8, NIV).

Lord, as I meditate on these words that were spoken to Moses so many
years ago, I fast forward to the birth of Jesus when you fulfilled a
similar promise. You looked upon the people you created and said, "I
have seen the misery of my people. I have heard them crying out. I'm
concerned about their suffering, and I'm going to send them a Savior."

Then you came down in the form of your Son to rescue us. You
promised a good land, a land flowing with abundant blessings,
for all who receive your wonderful gift of salvation. Thank you for
seeing. Thank you for sending. And thank you for saving. You are a
compassionate, merciful God.

From what misery has God saved you?

December 25

GOOD NEWS

That night there were shepherds staying in the fields nearby, guarding their flocks of sheep. Suddenly, an angel of the Lord appeared among them, and the radiance of the Lord's glory surrounded them. They were terrified, but the angel reassured them. "Don't be afraid!" he said. "I bring you good news that will bring great joy to all people. The Savior—yes, the Messiah, the Lord—has been born today in Bethlehem, the city of David!" (Luke 2:8-11, NLT)

All glory to you, Jesus! You're my Savior, my King, my Messiah, my Lord, and it's my honor to worship you. I praise you and delight in you, because you're the good news that brings great joy to all people.

The good news is that you're just what the world needs right now: you're the one who calms fears, you're the one who brings peace, you're the one who gives hope, you're the one who offers life. The message isn't only for today; it's for every day. And I want to shout it far and wide! I adore you, Jesus. You bring me great joy.

How does the birth of Jesus bring you joy?

December 26

IN THE NEIGHBORHOOD

The Word became a human and lived among us. We saw his glory—
the glory that belongs to the only Son of the Father—and he was full
of grace and truth (John 1:14, NCV).

Jesus, I'm wowed by this thought. Many years ago, you—the almighty
God—took on flesh and blood and moved into the neighborhood. You
exhibited the characteristics of your Father, who is generous and full
of grace and truth. You did what you came to do, and then moved
back with your Father in heaven.

Another wow thought is that you gave the gift of your Spirit to all
who believe and trust in you. Your Spirit lives within me. That means
wherever I go in my neighborhood, I'm taking you along. May I
represent you well.

How do you feel about Jesus living in the neighborhood?

December 27

FOREVER AND EVER

"The LORD will reign forever and ever!" (Exodus 15:18, NLT)

Hallelujah!

After pondering these words, what's your response?

December 28

THE WAY OF LIFE

You will show me the way of life,
granting me the joy of your presence
and the pleasures of living with you forever (Psalm 16:11, NLT).

In your presence is fullness of joy. In your presence are eternal pleasures. In your presence is life.

Thank you for showing me the way to you. Lord, open my heart and my mind to your presence. I want to receive and experience all you have for me today and throughout eternity. May I delight in you as you delight in me.

What do you experience in God's presence?

December 29

HE LEADS THE BLIND

"I will lead the blind by ways they have not known,
along unfamiliar paths I will guide them;
I will turn the darkness into light before them
and make the rough places smooth.
These are the things I will do;
I will not forsake them" (Isaiah 42:16, NIV).

Lord, so much of my life is unknown. I don't know what tomorrow
holds. I don't know what the rest of today holds. But I know you, and
that's enough. When things come into my life that are out of the
ordinary, you'll show me what to do. You'll hold my hand. Thank you
for the reassurance that my unfamiliar paths are not unfamiliar to you.

I praise you for being my almighty God who can do amazing and
impossible things. I praise you for your guidance and your ability to
turn darkness into light. Thank you for going before me and making
the rough places smooth. You're my faithful, trustworthy God. I'm
grateful my life is in your hands.

What unfamiliar paths are you facing right now?

December 30

RESURRECTION AND LIFE

Jesus said to her, "I am the resurrection and the life. The one who believes in me will live, even though they die; and whoever lives by believing in me will never die. Do you believe this?"
(John 11:25-26, NIV)

Jesus, you take the fear out of death. Every man and woman will one day die, and none of us has a say about the timing. But one thing's for sure—you are the resurrection and the life. If I believe in you and put my trust in you, I will live. Forever. With you.

Not only do I have your promise of eternal life, you also promise me new life and abundant life. Today. In you. To make things even better, you sent your Holy Spirit to reside in me and teach me how to live the best way. Every day. For you. I praise you for being all about life. Thank you for making it possible for me.

How does Jesus' statement that he is the resurrection and the life impact you?

December 31

ALWAYS THE SAME

Jesus Christ is the same yesterday and today and forever
(Hebrews 13:8, NIV).

I exalt you, Lord Jesus, for you never change.

You are the same yesterday, today, and forever.

As I end this year and start a fresh year tomorrow,

help me remember that yesterday, today, and forever you are...

Jesus, my Savior

Immanuel, God with me

Messiah

Wonderful Counselor

Mighty God

Everlasting Father

Prince of Peace

I AM

You were all I needed yesterday. You are all I need today. And you'll
be everything I need tomorrow. I praise your holy, magnificent name!

As you reflect on the past year, how has the never-changing
Jesus been everything you need?